UNCOVERING
Traditional
QUILTS

ADVENTURES IN PIECING

 American Quilter's Society
P. O. Box 3290 • Paducah, KY 42002-3290
www.AQSquilt.com

Joyce
Jones

Located in Paducah, Kentucky, the American Quilter's Society (AQS) is dedicated to promoting the accomplishments of today's quilters. Through its publications and events, AQS strives to honor today's quilt-makers and their work and to inspire future creativity and innovation in quiltmaking.

EDITOR: MARJORIE L. RUSSELL
GRAPHIC DESIGNER: TOM SULLIVAN
COVER DESIGNER: MICHAEL BUCKINGHAM
CARTOONIST: MICHAEL BUCKINGHAM
PHOTOGRAPHER: JEFF MEIN SMITH

Library of Congress Cataloging-in-Publication Data

Jones, Joyce.
    Uncovering traditional quilts : Adventures in Piecing / Joyce Jones.
               p. cm.
    ISBN 1-57432-758-5
    1. Patchwork--Patterns. 2. Patchwork quilts--New Zealand.   I. Title.
TT835.J66 2001
746.46'041--dc21   2001001606
                                                CIP

Additional copies of this book may be ordered from the American Quilter's Society, PO Box 3290, Paducah, KY 42002-3290, or online at www.AQSquilt.com.

A decade ago, Joyce Jones began designing stunning and seemingly complex quilt blocks using a few simple units. It was not a novel concept – time managers routinely advise busy executives to slice their big projects up into bite-sized pieces. However, when applied to quilt block construction, new and complex-looking designs emerged from these very simple units.

Working first with pencil and paper, then with her computer, Joyce found she could rotate, mirror, flip – in fact, do many things to these units to create new and exciting block designs. And unexpected secondary design bonuses emerged when the blocks were placed together. Quite apart from the time savings achieved by chain piecing many identical units, the step-by-step process also enabled even relatively inexperienced quilters to enjoy the excitement and thrill of creating their own blocks.

Joyce simplified and refined her techniques, then shared her designs with a dedicated group of quilters ranging from beginners to experienced. Serendipity played its part in the process, and spare units left over from blocks were quickly utilized in original new border designs.

Literally hundreds of quilts have been designed and made using these techniques. Each quilt is based on two simple methods yielding 16 different units, and these units can be rearranged endlessly. Simple changes in value and color totally transform the designs, creating new and exciting possibilities.

Uncovering Traditional Quilts: Adventures in Piecing opens new vistas for quilters who like traditional block-based quilts but wish to give those designs their own twist. Practical, simple, and exciting, the technique will set quilters on a new and adventurous path. The sky's the limit – take the time to play with these simple units and enjoy your newfound creativity!

Anne Scott
Editor & Publisher
New Zealand Quilter magazine

Table of Contents

UNCOVERING
TRADITIONAL QUILTS

Kiwi Feathers

ADVENTURES
IN PIECING

Table of Contents

I n t r o d u c t i o n

It seems that everything done by women must be repeated on a daily basis. Washing, driving kids to school, cooking, cleaning, shopping, working, and meeting the needs of children, husbands, parents – the list goes on. But, who is remembered for clean floors, or a tidy house, or for being a good housekeeper?

When women quilt, we emerge from the shadowy area of daily tasks to create a thing of lasting beauty, an heirloom to be handed down to future generations. When a woman makes a quilt, it may be the first time her family recognizes her for a talent other than that of keeping a good home.

To me, quilting offers a sense of order, precision and never-ending variety. I have also come to persuade myself that I am, after all, not that bad at math or color and have more patience than I ever dreamed possible.

For years I bought fabric, washed it and stored it, taking it out occasionally to drool over it before putting it back on the shelf, as Elinor Peace Bailey says in her poem *Play*, "for someone, more clever than I, to make a masterpiece!" It was many years before I finally had the courage to cut into that ever-increasing stash.

It is not by reading books, poring over patterns, or talking about quilting that a masterpiece is made. Rather, it is accomplished by actually cutting fabric and daring to do something with it – by taking chances, by making changes, by simply doing! To possess fabric is only the begin-

MARBLE MOUNTAIN

ning. To do something magical with it is our *raison d'etre* for spending that money in the first place! Or it should be, I tell myself!

Uncovering Traditional Quilts will encourage you to cut into your collection, by offering original designs that can be made without fuss. Have you ever looked at a quilt, or the picture of a quilt, and fallen totally in love with it? Then when you studied the detail, or maybe even tried to read the pattern, you thought, "Oh no, I couldn't do that!" or "It's too hard for me!"

Every quilt in *Uncovering Traditional Quilts* has been designed using Squirty and Squiffy units. Don't let the names cause you any consternation. Squirty and Squiffy are a form of quilting shorthand that gets easier and more fun every time you use it. You can actually "talk" your way through a quilt using the language of Squirty and Squiffy. But you don't have to speak the language in order to make the quilts in this book, the instructions for each quilt are quite clear.

As you learn to identify Squirty and Squiffy elements, you will build confidence in analyzing blocks and the units in them. I hope that you will also get the courage to construct your own blocks by learning to play with, change, and mix the units.

The original quilts in this book may look complicated, but they are so simple to construct. MARBLE MOUNTAIN was Carolyn McKay's second quilt. After doing a workshop on the Squirty and Squiffy techniques, I suggested to Carolyn that she could make MARBLE MOUNTAIN if she could "talk" through the block. Up until then, her one quilting achievement was a lap-sized Churn Dash quilt. She named all the units in MARBLE MOUNTAIN's block and, without thinking, said, "Oh, that's easy!" MARBLE MOUNTAIN was time-consuming because the blocks have a lot of pieces, but it was easy! Carolyn's lovely border uses bonus units made during the construction of the quilt.

It has been a joy watching our quilt group, The UnderCover Girls, grow and sustain one another with tolerance, humor, caring, and increasing talent. Many members of the group have gone from being totally timid beginners to quilters of real ability.

It is difficult to explain the incredible support The UnderCover Girls have given me in my endeavors. When I wanted to give up, they cheered me on. And best of all, they made the quilts for this book! So many times, they completely changed something midstream because I felt it would look better than the way we had started. They gave me their trust, and their "all," for which I feel very humble.

The UnderCover Girls are sure you will enjoy the excitement and adventure of making the quilts in *Uncovering Traditional Quilts*. When you do, it will be thanks to:

Nan Batty, Kath Beresford, Pat Buchanan, Alison Crawford, Anne Day, Marion Dixon, Bev Dyke (machine quilting), Betty Gilbert, Carol Greig, Becky Hamilton, Carolyn McKay, Jill Raine, Elaine Wright, and Lois Zachariassen.

I also want to thank part-time Nelsonian, inspirational friend, and contributing quilter to *Uncovering Traditional Quilts*, quilt artist Rhoda Cohen of Boston, Massachusetts.

Rhoda's treatment of one of my designs transformed it into her own unique piece of fabric art. Her inimitable approach to quilting showers

PERPETUAL MOTION

those around her with mind-expanding, talent-extending enthusiasm for the unexpected. I still cannot believe she let me talk her into using a rotary cutter – for the first and last time!

Inspirational too was the artistic input of photographer Jeff Mein Smith of Wakefield, Nelson, New Zealand. Jeff brought his talents to the task of photographing the quilts for this book. As quilters, we couldn't see past chairs, beds, and walls. Not so Jeff! He brought excitement and flair to everything he did. Avid quilters need not worry about the apparent abandon in the photography – every quilt was treated with care and respect. Jeff's aim was to make *Uncovering Traditional Quilts* graphically interesting to quilters and non-quilters alike.

The name of our machine quilter, Bev Dyke, is repeated frequently in *Uncovering Traditional Quilts*. Many of the quilters relied on Bev's talents to add the final touch, and she helped with ideas of how and where to quilt. Nothing was too much trouble if that was what the quilt needed. Just try having groups of quilters leave their "babies" in your hands – it's a quick way to have your quilting talents pushed to their limits!

I know you will enjoy the process and fun of working through the many traditional-style original quilts within these pages.

This book is dedicated to my soul-mate, Ted, for his patience and support, for being Mr. Fix-It, and head chef, and for believing in me – bless you!

Joyce Jones

Arohanui (with love to all)
A New Zealand Maori greeting

Dear Quiltmaker:

From our earliest children's books to swashbuckling adventure movies, we admire those with the courage to enter into unfamiliar territory and emerge victorious. As the hero moves from one tense scene to another in pursuit of a treasured goal, we get caught up in the story, experiencing the thrill of adventure from the safety of a theater seat or a comfortable chair at home.

Quiltmaking is also an adventure that we sometimes observe from a safe distance. While we may admire those who courageously cut and piece their way through the jungles of quiltmaking, it seems safer to stick with the familiar. But, adventures in piecing quilts don't have to belong to someone else. The victory of a fantastic quilt can belong to **you**.

Faraway places with exotic names offer you choices of adventures in piecing traditional quilts. TASMAN BAY, TRAFALGAR SQUARE, FIFESHIRE, D'URVILLE, KOWHAI – the names themselves stimulate imagination and stir excitement. They could be locations for a modern Indiana Jones or Star Wars movies!

Join the adventure! Accompany two seasoned heroes of piecing as they uncover the hidden treasures, exotic corners, adventure, and excitement in your traditional quilts. And who are these heroes! Not Indiana Jones, not Robin Hood, not Nancy Drew or the Hardy Boys – meet Squirty and Squiffy!

New Zealand resident and author Joyce Jones has developed, sewn, and shared the secrets of Squirty and Squiffy for years. Like other successful teachers, such as the legendary Doreen Speckmann who use cartoon characters as part of the teaching process, Joyce has chosen Squirty and Squiffy to illuminate her methods. They are the adventurers who will guide you to amazing discoveries within your own quilts. Using innovative shortcuts and a shorthand language that helps identify both piece and process, Squirty and Squiffy will add new zing to your quilts.

Whether or not you learn the language of Squirty and Squiffy, you can still make the quilts in this book. Delightfully easy, Joyce's method will produce stunning heirloom-quality quilts.

Let the adventures begin!

Marjorie L. Russell
Editor, American Quilter's Society

Squiffy   **Squirty**

Squirty

Our friend Squirty, is a pieced square unit composed of two, three, or four triangles: Tri-2, a half-square triangle unit; Tri-4, a quarter-square triangle unit; and Tri-3, a combination of both. Squirty is a structural element; his units are part of the basic quilt design, as opposed to something added on later.

Squiffy

By contrast, Squiffy is an add-on adventurer. Her job is to change the appearance of a base cut piece. Employing the corner-square method, Squiffy squares are stitched with a diagonal seam onto larger squares or rectangles (and even to finished blocks), then are folded over to form corner triangles.

Squirty Square Family

Squares into Triangles

TRI-2

TRI-4

TRI-3

Squirty Square Family

Squirty Square identifies both the appearance and the process of constructing a family of pieced triangle units. This technique has been widely used for some time now. I started using it at least 10 years ago and thought it was all my own idea! Is anything, ever?

There are three units in the Squirty Square family: Tri-2, Tri-3, and Tri-4. These names are logical explanations of the units and their construction.

There are many ways to capitalize on varying sizes of any Squirty Square triangle units. Refer to the Quick Calculations chart on page 11.

The size quilt you make often alters the size block you need. A larger quilt may look better with slightly larger blocks. For example, you may have seen a lovely Ohio Star quilt and want to make something similar in a different size. To get the width you need may require seven 10" blocks, or ten 7" blocks. Using the chart allows you to alter the size of the blocks rather than making a lot more blocks.

As you go through the quilts in *Uncovering Traditional Quilts*, you will naturally work to the sizes listed for each quilt. To get used to the construction of these units, "Let's Try It!" on the next page will take you, step-by-step through making four-inch finished samples of each Squirty square unit.

Marking and Assembling Squirty Squares

(Read "Aids to Accuracy," page 26, before marking or sewing)

1. Place the ¼" line of your ruler corner to corner and draw a thin, sharp pencil or soap line. Turn and repeat on the other side. With right sides together, sew on the seam allowance side of the drawn line. Check the seams, cut between sewn lines and press open. This method is excellent if your machine does not have a ¼" foot **OR,**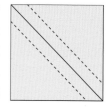

2. Draw a line from corner to corner. Sew ¼" on both sides of the line. Check seams before cutting on the line and pressing open.

 Learn to identify the Squirty Square units as shown. "Talk" them to yourself – Tri-2, Tri-3, Tri-4. (See "Talking the Talk," page 21). Whenever you see one of the units, repeat its name. If you were describing it to someone, what would you say? Would you say it was a square made of four triangles? Perhaps. But, why not describe it as a Tri-4? That says it all.

 Each set of Tri-3s produces mirror image units (see page 11). Some blocks use left or right units, others use both. Learn which ones you need! In some cases, this could mean you have a whole heap of left or right surplus units. Nothing need be wasted! There are wonderful borders that can be made using single or mirror image Tri-3s (see page 20 for more on Bonus Tri-2s).

Squirty Squares . . . LET'S TRY IT!

TRI-2 – Quick Calculations • Cut one light and one dark square ⅞" larger than finished size.

 To make a 4" finished Tri-2, cut one light 4⅞" square and one dark 4⅞" square. Draw a line corner to corner on the wrong side of the light square.

 With right sides together, position the light square on top of the dark square. Sew a scant ¼" on both sides of the drawn line. Check the seams for accuracy. Cut between the seam lines and press open.

 Makes two 4" finished Tri-2 units.

TRI-3 – Quick Calculations • Cut one light and one dark square 1¼" larger than finished size, and one medium square ⅞" larger than finished size.

 To make a 4" finished Tri-3, cut one light 5¼" square, one dark 5¼" square, and two medium 4⅞" squares. Draw a line corner to corner on the wrong side of the light square. Position dark and light squares with right sides together.

 Sew a scant ¼" on both sides of the drawn line. Cut between the seam lines to make two Tri-2 units.

 Then put each Tri-2 unit right sides together with a medium square. Draw a line from opposite corner to corner. Sew a scant ¼" on both sides of the drawn line, check, cut, and press.

    This yields four 4" finished Tri-3 units.

TRI-4 – Quick Calculations • Cut one light and one dark square 1¼" larger than finished size.

 To make a 4" finished Tri-4, cut one light 5¼" square and one dark 5¼" square.

 Make Tri-2 units using light and dark squares.

 Then position two Tri-2 units right sides together but in reverse alignment so dark matches light, and the seams butt well together. Mark from corner to opposite corner.

 Sew a scant ¼" on both sides of the drawn line, check, cut, and press.

 This will yield two 4" finished Tri-4 units.

Squiffy Square Family

Squares added to form Triangles

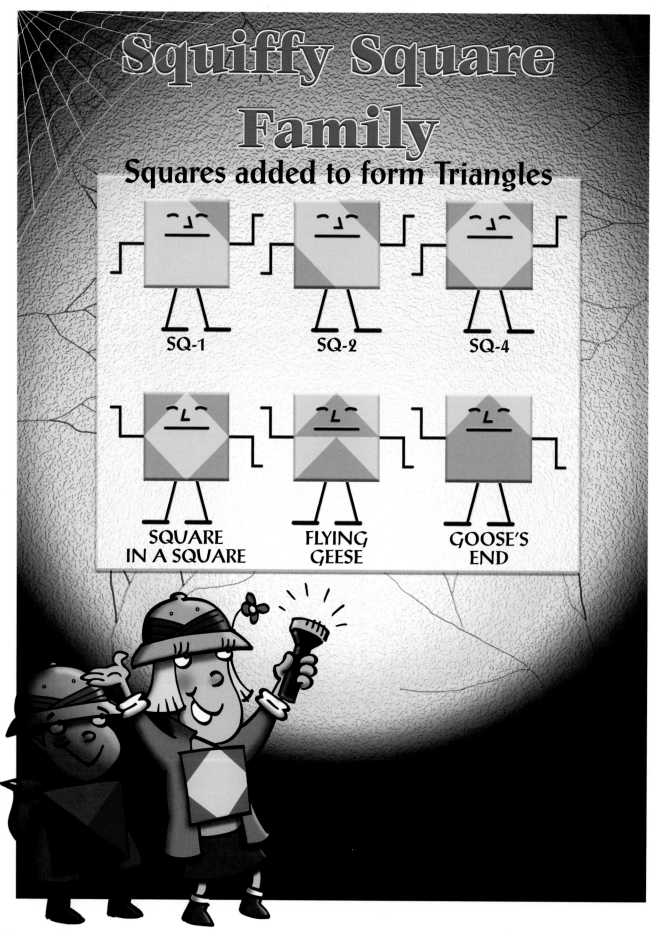

SQ-1

SQ-2

SQ-4

SQUARE
IN A SQUARE

FLYING
GEESE

GOOSE'S
END

Squiffy Square Family

The fabulous, versatile Squiffy square! These wonderful squares, added to squares or rectangles, have proven so helpful in construction, so helpful in giving variety to blocks, and have even been helpful in narrowly avoiding a couple of near disasters in mystery quilts.

One mystery quilt I was involved in was so boring that I was tempted not to finished it (another UFO hidden for posterity to find). But, while analyzing the quilt during the block stage, I found that by adding Squiffy squares I could change the whole feel of the quilt. The best part of adding Squiffies was that I didn't have to un-sew – I simply added them to the existing blocks.

There are a number of cousins, second cousins, and even a couple of pets in the Squiffy family. You'll enjoy getting to know the possibilities and versatility of these little units.

Because they are sewn from corner to corner, Squiffy squares are a seam allowance smaller than conventional triangle pieces. They also don't have the seam allowance "hang-over" associated with other methods of sewing triangles. Squiffy squares attach with ease and are much less of a hassle than trying to attach an already cut angle.

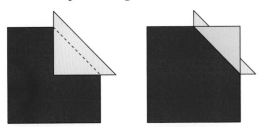

Conventional method with seam allowance "hang-over."

Squiffy square attaches with ease. No "hang-over."

Squiffy squares can be lifesavers in many situations. Whether you are referring to the corners of a block or a way to make sashing look terrific . . .

- Squiffy squares are simple
- Squiffy squares are accurate
- Squiffy squares are economical
- Squiffy squares are extremely adaptable
- Squiffy squares add zest to sashing and border designs
- Squiffy squares offer a bonus of ready-made triangle units
- Squiffy squares are totally user friendly, and best of all...
- Squiffy squares waste no more fabric than using templates or other cutting methods.

Everything Joyce says is true.

I'm a wonderful gal from a good family!

Base Cut Pieces

This is a square or rectangle piece cut the full size required with no corners trimmed off where a pre-cut triangle will be added. A good example of this piece is Flying Geese where the base cut piece is a rectangle, the full size of the area to be occupied.

Squares are added to the rectangle, sewn, and trimmed, to form triangles at either end. The original base cut is the exact size needed for that section of the block, so what can go wrong? Sure, if you are careless when adding the squares, you could have a problem. But you wouldn't do that, would you?

Marking and Assembling Squiffy Squares

Size Squiffies according to the requirements of your design. Draw a pencil or fine soap line from corner to corner of each square every time you add a Squiffy square (see "Aids to Accuracy," pg. 26). Place the square with right sides together on the corner of the base unit. Sew on the seam allowance side of the line. Flip up the bottom corner of the Squiffy square and finger press it in half to form a triangle. If the corners don't match, before cutting check your sewn line for accuracy. Unpick and re-sew if necessary.

Before trimming the Squiffy square to a ¼" seam allowance, decide if you want to save the small Bonus Tri-2 formed by the corner (see page 20 for Bonus Tri-2 directions). In fact, if you decide to keep it, save time by marking another line ½" from the first before starting to sew. Then stitch to the seam allowance side of both lines and cut between the two.

Squiffy Squares . . . LET'S TRY IT!

Squiffy Square One (Sq-1) – This is an excellent unit for blocks such as Bow Tie and is ideal for changing the corners of blocks.

 Cut 1 dark 4½" square and 1 light 2½" square. Draw a line, corner to corner, on the wrong side of the 2½" square; draw a second line ½" to the right of the first line, if you would like to save the small Bonus Tri-2 (see Bonus Tri-2, pg. 20).

 With right sides together, position the 2½" square in the upper right corner of the 4½" square. Sew to the seam allowance side of both lines. Finger press the corner up to make certain the edges match.

 Cut between the lines.

 Yields a finished 4" Sq-1 and one finished 1¼" Bonus Tri-2 unit.

Squiffy Squares . . . LET'S TRY IT! (continued)

Squiffy Square Two (Sq-2) – This is an excellent unit for using scraps to make blocks such as Kansas Dugout, Indian Hatchet, and others, or for changing corner units in other blocks.

  Cut 1 dark 4½" square and 2 light 2½" squares. Draw a line, corner to corner, on the wrong sides of the 2½" squares; draw a second line ½" to the right of the first line for the Bonus Tri-2s.

 With right sides together, position a 2½" square in the upper right corner of the 4½" square. Sew to the seam allowance side of both lines. Finger press the corner up to make certain the edges match. Rotate the square and attach the second 2½" square to the opposite corner.

 Cut between the lines.

  Yields a 4" finished Sq-2 and two finished 1½" bonus Tri-2s.

Squiffy Square Four (Sq-4) – Snowball – The corner Squiffies can vary in size to match the block they adjoin.

Cut 1 dark 6½" square and 4 light 2½" squares. Draw a line, corner to corner, on the wrong sides of the 2½" squares; draw a second line ½" from the first.

 With right sides together, position a 2½" square in the upper right corner of the 6½" square. The second drawn line should be closest to the corner. Sew to the seam allowance side of each line. Finger press the corner up to make certain the edges match.

 Cut between the two lines. Rotate the large square, attaching the remaining squares in the same manner.

Yields one finished 6" Sq-4 (Snowball) unit plus four 1½" bonus Tri-2s. This Snowball will match a 6" finished Nine-patch perfectly.

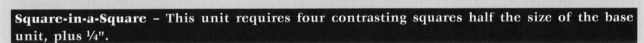

Square-in-a-Square – This unit requires four contrasting squares half the size of the base unit, plus ¼".

 Cut 1 dark 6½" square and 4 light 3½" squares. Draw a line from corner to corner on the wrong side of each small square; draw a second line ½" from the first for the Bonus Tri-2 units.

 With right sides together, position a 3½" square in the upper right corner of the 6½" square. Sew to the seam allowance side of both lines. Check to make certain the edges match. Attach a second Squiffy square to the opposite corner, check, trim and press back.

  Add squares to the last two opposing corners; check, cut, and press back.

   Yields a finished 6" Square-in-a-Square unit plus four finished 2¼" Bonus Tri-2s.

Versatile Sq-1s and Sq-2s

Want to make an Ohio Star? Try using Sq-2s in the corner units. For example, if each unit is 3", try a 2" Squiffy on both corners, or maybe a 2½" Squiffy in one corner and 1½" in the other. You could use the same fabric for both Squiffies or two different fabrics. See what pleases you – play!

You may decide you like just a Sq-1. Turn it so that the Squiffy is in the corner of the Ohio Star – turn it again so that it comes out to the corner of the block – this will make a connecting pattern when the blocks are sewn together.

Explore the options before sewing units together, changing units around until the results please you. Squiffy squares are so adaptable! Choose the size Squiffy you want to add, change the size, change your mind – no problem!

Add it later! Squiffy squares are something you can add after you have made your block or unit.

Take a completed block you are not very happy with and add a small Squiffy to one corner. Now add a larger Squiffy to another corner.

On another corner, put a large Squiffy first then a smaller one on top. Layering Squiffies is very effective, but it's wiser to do this when you plan to use sashing. Double Squiffy corners need a little more care when sewing the blocks together without the sashing.

When changing a unit or a block by adding a Squiffy, it gives you a chance to look at the result and see whether you like it or not. Always do this before sewing the Bonus Tri-2 line and cutting. If you don't like the result, just unpick and remove – the base cut piece is still the same as when you started.

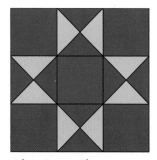

Ohio Star – Plain

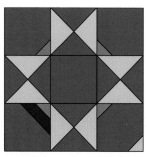

Ohio Star with Sq-1s and layered Squiffies

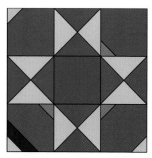

Ohio Star with Sq-2s and layered Squiffies

And Here Come Squiffy Square's Cousins and Second Cousins, "The Recs!"

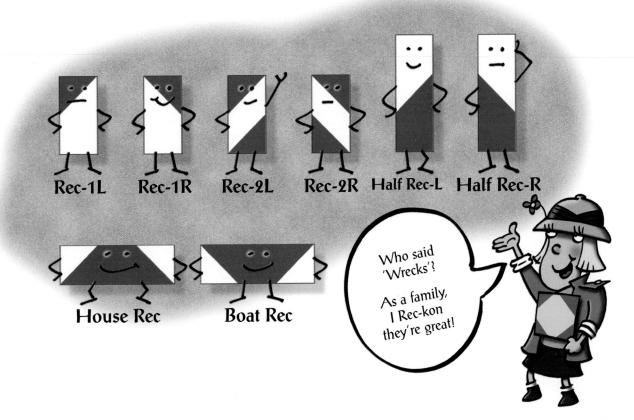

Rec-1L   Rec-1R   Rec-2L   Rec-2R   Half Rec-L   Half Rec-R

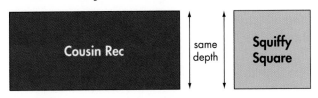

House Rec   Boat Rec

Who said 'Wrecks'?

As a family, I Rec-kon they're great!

The Rec (short for Rectangle) cousins join with Squiffy squares to make wonderful and valuable units. Don't underestimate these Squiffy family members. Many of the most interesting designs in *Uncovering Traditional Quilts* have been designed with Rec units. And they're just as easy to work with as square units.

Understanding Right and Left Recs
Attached Squiffy squares are always the same size as the shortest side of a Rec – that makes it easy to remember.

Cousin Rec	same depth	Squiffy Square

Look at Rec-1L above – the dark triangle goes up to the left. Look at the next unit Rec-

1R – the dark triangle goes up to the right. Whichever way you turn the unit, the angle remains the same. You can't get mixed up even when you turn the unit to add another Squiffy.

House and Boat Recs are the Squiffy family's second cousins – both have one square flipped to the left, the other to the right. While the UnderCover Girls were working with these units, we wanted a special name for them because they are a different kind of Rec-2. We had been making some house blocks and another student was making a boat quilt. It was obvious that the unit used for the roof of the house became the hull of a boat when turned upside down. For ease of identification, these units simply had to be called House Recs or Boat Recs.

Assembling the Recs . . . LET'S TRY IT!

REC-1L

Cut one 4½" x 2½" rectangle and a 2½" square. Draw a line corner to corner on the wrong side of the 2½" square. With right sides together as shown, attach the 2½" square to the rectangle. Fold the square back to ensure it will go up to the left. Trim, leaving a ¼" seam allowance.

REC-1R

Cut one 4½" x 2½" rectangle and a 2½" square. Draw a line corner to corner on the wrong side of the 2½" square. Attach Squiffy as above, but with the angle to the right.

REC-2L

Cut one 4½" x 2½" rectangle and two 2½" squares. Begin as for Rec-1L. After attaching the first Squiffy turn the rectangle and repeat. Trim, leaving a ¼" seam allowance.

REC-2R

Cut one 4½" x 2½" rectangle and two 2½" squares. Draw a line corner to corner on wrong sides of the 2½" squares. Begin as for Rec-1R. After attaching the first Squiffy, turn the rectangle and repeat. Trim, leaving a ¼" seam allowance.

HALF REC-L

Cut two 4½" x 2½" rectangles, one light and one dark. Place the light Rec on the dark in the position shown, with right sides together. Draw a line from the top left corner of the light (the line should finish level with the corner of the Rec underneath. Check before sewing. Trim, leaving a ¼" seam allowance.

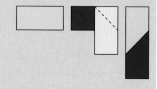

HALF REC-R

Cut two 4½" x 2½" rectangles, one light and one dark. Place light Rec on the dark as shown. Mark and attach Squiffy as for Half Rec-L.

Whenever you use these units, always check before sewing to make certain you have the direction you want.

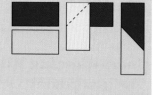

HOUSE REC

Cut one 6½" x 2½" rectangle and two 2½" squares. Begin as for Rec-1L then turn and attach the second square to go to the right. Simply turn a House Rec over to make a Boat Rec.

BOAT REC

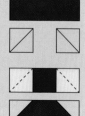

Family Pets – The Squiffy Geese . . . LET'S TRY IT!

Squiffy Geese – This ratio applies to any size Flying Geese unit. Whatever the length of the Rec, the depth of the Rec and squares must be half the length, plus ¼".

SQUIFFY GEESE

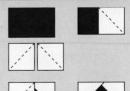

Cut one dark 6½" x 3½" rectangle and two light 3½" squares. On the squares, draw a line from corner to corner. Place a square on the right side of the Rec, with right sides together as shown. Sew on the seam allowance side of the line. Check for accuracy. Trim and press back to form a triangle. Attach the second Squiffy on the other side in the same manner.

Note that the second Squiffy overlaps the first slightly to provide the seam allowance. Also, when sewing Squiffy Geese to another unit, take a fractionally narrower seam to avoid point pinching.

Samples – Finished Squiffy Geese Units

Finished unit	Cut 1 Rec	Cut 2 Squiffies
6" x 3"	6½" x 3½"	3½"
5½" x 2¾"	6" x 3¼"	3¼"
4½" x 2¼"	5" x 2¾"	2¾"

Remember, bonus Tri-2s are always worthwhile on Squiffy squares 2½" or larger (see pg. 20).

Goose's End – Look for this unit when you are analyzing blocks. It is made the same way as Squiffy Geese but with a larger base unit.

GOOSE'S END

Cut one dark 4½" square and two light 2½" squares. Use the same procedure as for any Flying Geese unit, checking for accuracy before cutting apart and pressing.

In VINTAGE NELSON (pg. 53), note the use of this unit, in alternating light and dark, in the block and especially the border.

Versatile Rec-2s

Have a look at the quilt block Aunt Sukey's Choice at the right that contains Flying Geese units. There are two different ways to make those units. One is using two Flying Geese units – one with dark corners, the other with light corners.

Aunt Sukey's Choice – Flying Geese

A second very effective alternative is to use two Rec-2 units, one a Rec-2L, and the other a Rec-2R. By using two different value fabrics, you can achieve an interesting three-dimensional effect in your blocks.

Aunt Sukey's Choice – Rec-2s

The Family's Influence Expands

Sashing

There are many ways to use Squiffy squares to add interest to sashing. The next time you're sashing a quilt, consider adding Squiffy squares to each end of the sashing to form stars.

Star effect

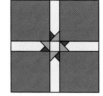
Tri-3 effect

Or add a second Squiffy square in the opposite direction over the first to make a Tri-3. The sashing can look like another connecting block for a great effect!

Pieced Inner Borders

Use the same Squiffy methods to add interest to an inner border. The simple addition of Squiffy squares to inner borders can "finish off" the stars that have been used in sashing blocks. Examples can be seen in LIVE IN HOPE (pg. 40), TRAFALGAR SQUARE (pg. 107) and others in this book.

Bonus Triangles

Wherever possible, take advantage of the bonus triangles created when adding Squiffies to squares or rectangles. It is very simple to draw a second line when adding a Squiffy, and sew on the second line to create a bonus Tri-2 unit. The only time it may not be worth making bonus Tri-2s is when the Squiffy you are using is 2" or less in size.

Most often the bonus triangles will be Tri-2s, but some units yield Tri-3s or Tri-4 bonuses. MARBLE MOUNTAIN on page 84 is a good example of this. There is no waste of fabric in MARBLE MOUNTAIN because all but a few of the border Tri-4s are a by-product of the quilt blocks themselves. Imagine while you are piecing a block, you are gaining ready-made

bonus Tri-4s for a stunning border. When contemplating a pieced border, a big plus is that you do not have to start making endless small units. They are already made!

Occasionally, you might know that you will not want to use the bonus triangles in the quilt you are currently making. Don't let that stop you from sewing and saving. I have seen lovely small quilts and wallhangings made from bonus triangle units saved from other quilts. You'll never have to wonder what to do if you have a box full of Tri-2s waiting to trimmed, ready for use.

Making Bonus Tri-2s

Draw a second line, a half-inch from the first line on your Squiffy square. Always sew directly on, but to the seam allowance edge of both lines before cutting. This helps to maintain accuracy of the smaller bonus units. If you cut the triangles off before sewing, it is almost a guarantee you will never get around to sewing them later.

Several of the quilts in this book use a ⅜" space between the two lines rather than the normal ½" to allow for a slightly larger bonus unit. This can make all the difference so make sure you test the first few bonus Tri-2s to ensure you are getting the size required. When cutting between the two lines, leave a full ¼" for the main unit, with the smaller seam allowance for the bonus Tri-2. Never press these smaller seams open.

To foil the forces of the Bland Border People, Squiffy makes a few quick calculations. Together she and partner, Squirty, produce an army of Bonus Tri-2 family members to secure the perimeter.

Trimming Bonus Tri-2s

Here are some ways to help cut down frustration and get the results you want.

• Be as careful as you can in marking and sewing each bonus Tri-2, and be consistent in the needle distance in relation to the drawn line.

• Press gently or finger press so as not to distort the units.

• Use a small square ruler to trim the units. The ruler should have a 45° angle, and ⅛" markings for squares. Rulers with fine line squares are preferable because it is difficult to be as accurate using heavy-lined rulers. Be consistent in your placement of the ruler.

• Place each Tri-2 with the dark corner consistently to the left. Put the diagonal line of the ruler so that it is in line with the diagonal line of your Tri-2 unit.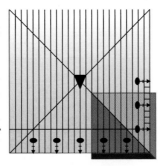

• Make sure that the left and top edges of the unit (which get trimmed in the second cut) don't come inside the line for the size square you desire. Trim the excess off the bottom and right sides.

• Turn the unit 180° and line up the freshly cut sides with the measurement you want. Trim the excess, if any, off the bottom and right sides. Before cutting, always make sure the diagonal line of your ruler matches the diagonal line of the unit. This ensures that the Tri-2s match perfectly when sewn together.

• It pays to trim the bonus Tri-2s as you work to avoid a monumental task in the final stages. There will be some variation in the sizes you start with, so I suggest you find an average size and trim the squares to that size. Wherever bonus triangles are used in this book, the correct trimming sizes are given.

Quilting Shorthand
Talking the Talk

Learning to talk the language of Squiffy and Squirty makes the process of using them so much easier! It will stand you in good stead, not just for the quilts in this book, but also when you come to make quilts from other sources.

You will learn to analyze blocks, adjust sizing, change units, and have fun. The possibilities are endless and very exciting. But the first step is to learn the language. Initially, it may take a little effort and will result in a few laughs, but the more you "talk" the process, the better and easier it will get. You and your friends will soon be talking in Quilting Shorthand.

Here's an example:
You: "I'm thinking of doing an Ohio Star quilt. It's my favorite block. I'll need four Tri-4s, a center square, and maybe four Tri-2s in the corners."

Friend: "What if you used Sq-2s in the corners? Or maybe Sq-1s using different fabric. It would give a nice corner interest."

You: "Mmmm – or even two different size Squiffies on the Sq-2s. I'll try that."

Anyone listening might think you're from Mars, but this Quilting Shorthand cuts right through all the problems of explaining what you want, especially to yourself. Try it! It works!

"It doesn't do to leave a live dragon out of your calculations!"
~ J. R. R. Tolkein

Dragon Tamers

With the best will in the world and the most meticulous care in cutting and sewing, there can still be the odd dragon – something that requires an unexpected design treatment – lurking, just waiting to make its presence felt. Don't be too hard on that dragon for often it will cause you to make changes that really improve the quilt. Many one-of-a-kind quilts are unique because of the odd dragon. But, a whole horde of dragons is another thing.

Squiffy squares can tame many of the dragons we come up against because they eliminate potential errors found when cutting triangles and attaching those triangles to cut pieces. An example of this is the common Snowball patch. Try making one Snowball patch by the conventional method, and another using Squiffy squares, and I'm certain you will prefer the latter. I often hear, "I wish I had known about Squiffy squares before I made my Snowball and Nine-Patch quilt."

Piecing Tips

Find time to make all the units shown in this book – possibly from scraps. Where possible, aim for a common size using the Quick Calculations (pg. 11). It is stimulating to sit with a whole pile of units and let your imagination run wild. The "what-ifs" are endless. If you come up with a block you really like, use two mirrors to see what multiples of the block will offer.

Perfect ¼" Seams

Place a piece of fairly wide masking tape from just clear of the feed dogs down to the edge of the tray. Using your quilting ruler, draw lines on the tape at ¼" spaces. The first should be in line with the needle, the other lines should be ¼" on either side of that line.

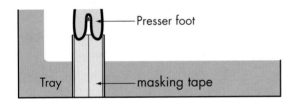

When you do not have a ¼" presser foot, the marked line to the right of the needle is an excellent guide for perfect ¼" seams.

Experienced quilters will find this tape a time-saving feature. Small Squiffy squares can be sewn without marking. The illustration shows how to align the Squiffy under the needle. 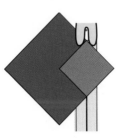 As you sew, the Squiffy square should stay in line with the center mark. Practice makes perfect with this non-marking method. Larger squares cover this line and always require marking. As always, keeping edges in alignment is most important.

Some Cutting Remarks

In the charts giving instructions for cutting are two categories listed as 1st cut and 2nd cut.

This means that when you are cutting fabric for more than one block, the first cut usually refers to the narrowest strip you will cut. For example, with units that are 2½" x 4½", the first cut will be a full width strip (or strips) 2½" by the full width of the fabric. The second cut will then be the 2½" strip cut into 4½" rectangles.

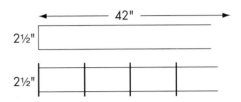

Start-a-Seam

Many of the designs in *Uncovering Traditional Quilts* use a construction method I call Start-a-Seam. I love blocks that use this method, as they appear to have more movement than others. They are also fun to construct.

Start-a-Seam is needed because the outer rectangle units are longer than the center unit. Sew the first seam to the halfway point as indicated by the Xs. This allows you to add each rectangular unit, going around the center in Log Cabin style.

Sew at least halfway down the seam, leave the needle in the "down" position, lift the foot, and turn the piece so you can sew "off the edge" straight onto your Threadle (see pg. 27). After sewing all four sides to the center square, start from the outer edge and complete the seam to the X near the center. Finish the same way you started, by sewing OFF the edge ONTO the Threadle.

The pattern will sometimes call for the Start-a-Seam to follow clockwise construction.

Auditioning

The first time I heard this word was in a Roberta Horton workshop, and it has stayed with me. Auditioning is an essential tool. If you've ever made a quilt and have not been really happy with the result, chances are that you planned and made the quilt strictly according to that plan, without letting the quilt have a say! Auditioning offers a chance for you to step back and let the quilt tell you what it needs. All you need to do is "listen."

When you've reached a point where the project isn't quite "jelling," step back from the quilt but don't put it out of sight. If possible, hang it where you can see it as you walk past. Let it surprise you as you come back into a room. Sometimes we are too close to what we are doing and need to take a few steps back.

Another great quilt teacher, Sharyn Craig, brought "what if?" into our quilting vocabularies. This is when you start saying to yourself, "What if I use a different fabric there, or maybe a different setting?" Give these "what-ifs" time to settle.

Fabrics you never thought would work may become the very thing the quilt needs. Always audition when you're not absolutely sure. Couple auditioning with "what if." These two essential quilting companions go hand-in-hand to produce the best results.

Color

Never let the color of a quilt put you off the design. Virtually without exception, color makes the first impression on us. If we don't feel comfortable with the colors the quilter has used, we often feel we don't like the quilt. Learn to see past the color to the design and use your imaginative gifts to visualize that same quilt in YOUR colors.

Even very ordinary designs can be totally charming if the color is good. Think about this and apply it next time you are not impressed with a quilt.

It is very helpful to study the quilts you don't like and find out why.

If you are having difficulty with color, try using several shades of each color rather than one of each. For example, if you have one dark red, one green, and one cream, try choosing several shades of the red, several of the green, and even more variety in cream.

A frequently-heard comment in classes, workshops, or other gatherings of quilters is, "I'm not very good with color!" This negative statement compounds the so-called problem. If you have ever heard yourself saying you are not good with color, learn to say instead, "I'm getting better with color!" Because you are! You are learning from everything you do. Every quilt you make teaches you more about color combinations, values, and more.

Don't be intimidated by color theorists. Everything each of us does with quilts, including the use of color, is not the only way, but is "our" way. That's what makes quilting such a wonderfully individual form of expression.

Value

Value, very simply put, is the darkness or lightness of a color. Changing the value can give a totally different personality to a quilt. This is well-illustrated by the Design Double Takes in this book. If you want to try an exercise on this theory, make up four or five Churn Dash blocks, altering values each time. You'll be surprised at the different visual impact of each block.

Visual Texture

Probably the single most effective way of bringing oomph and interest into a design is to use a good variety of visual textures.

Lack of visual texture tends to flatten even the best design. You can very effectively use three or more fabrics of the same color value but with different visual textures to add much more interest.

When adding to your stash, look for interesting changes of texture. Avoid buying two different colors with the same texture, if you intend to use them in the same quilt.

Visual texture can also play a critical role in borders. For example, a small inner border made from strips cut across the width of a striped fabric can be very effective.

Visual texture can be added to a quilt top by using graphically interesting quilting designs. Quilts with large, plain areas such as the border in BISHOPDALE (pg. 41) offer a showcase for quilters' talents.

Design Double Takes

Some of the fun The UnderCover Girls had with this collection came in analyzing the first quilt made from a particular design and then seeing how we could change the effect. Sometimes the results have been so drastic that other quilters have not realized that two quilts used the same block pattern but with different settings, different values, and different colors.

SANDY BAY (pg. 99) and TASMAN BAY (pg. 103) go from classic to scrap set on point to create a whole new atmosphere. Turn to page 79 and study KOWHAI before seeing the dramatic changes in COVER STORY and APPLEBY BLUES (pg. 83) made by bringing color from one block across into adjacent blocks.

BERRIED TREASURES

Getting a variety of effects from one design is not just a matter of changing colors, setting blocks on point, or adding sashing. The most noticeable changes come when you alter values. BERRIED TREASURES (pg. 36) and LIVE IN HOPE (pg. 40) are good examples.

VINTAGE NELSON (pg. 53) is a classic styling using positive/negative blocks, whereas D'URVILLE (pg. 49) uses scrap with a totally different border.

VINTAGE NELSON

D'URVILLE

SANDY BAY

TASMAN BAY

LIVE IN HOPE

The Eyes Have It!

Learn to "see" possible areas of difficulty before sewing units or blocks together.

Cut down on the time and nervous energy spent unsewing with the following suggestions:

• Use a Threadle (see pg. 27).

• Ensure that all edges of the squares to be sewn match and hold firmly together. Pin if you have to, but pins often distort more than help. Pinning in the opposite corner can help keep the fabrics aligned.

• Use a tailor's awl, stiletto or quick unpick (seam ripper) to hold the fabric together at the start and especially at the finish. Once you've taken the first 4–5 stitches, stop with the needle in the down position. Grasp the bottom of the seam line to be sewn, and hold the two squares firmly together. You may need to apply a little tension to ensure they meet squarely at the end. If you've made sure the fabric is together at the start and together at the finish of the seam, your piece will be accurate.

• If a point is lost in the sewing, unpick only a fraction to either side of the point and move it either backward or forward away from the other seam. Open the seam and look to see what is happening. Often only a tiny adjustment is needed to make it work. Unpicking the whole seam to fix something like this doesn't help. If the seams meet at the start and end of the sewing line, it is easier to fix a small segment of that sewing line by NOT unpicking the whole thing.

• You'll also soon learn to adjust when two 45° angles come together (or don't!). I'm always amazed to see how many times a student will unpick the same seam and keep sewing them together until the fabric becomes so tired it virtually collapses, and the student with it!

• Here's a psychological tool! Put aside any units that need adjustment, or blocks that aren't going well. Having learned what the problem is, go on to the next units or blocks. Wait until you have a cup of coffee in your hand or are sitting in front of the television to quietly unpick and determine how to re-sew for a better result.

Aids to Accuracy

Cutting: Measure, check, and check again before cutting. Many problems start with inaccurate cutting. When you put two squares together, if they don't match perfectly, find out where the problem is and fix it or cut new squares. Continuing only compounds the error.

Pencil lines: Use the side of a very sharp pencil to mark your fabric. This offers less drag and less chance of fraying the corner of the fabric. If your unit is not accurate, check how you are sewing on this line. There can be a surprising difference in the result depending upon whether you sew on the line, or with the needle fractionally to the seam allowance side of the marked line. A thick pencil line can cause havoc. Also, when marking dark fabric, fine, sharp slivers of soap do a great job. (The English brand, Imperial Leather, maintains a good, sharp edge. Treat the family and keep the end pieces for yourself.)

Assembly: When units or blocks fit badly, the main causes are:

1) Seams not being an accurate ¼" – there is a tendency for most quiltmakers to take narrower seams at both the start and end of seam lines (see "The Eyes Have It!", pg. 26, for remedies).

2) Edges not meeting – the bottom piece can often slip away from the top and not be noticed. Keep an eye on this as you sew.

3) Fabric uneven at the start or finish of the seam line (see "The Eyes Have It!").

4) Vigorous ironing or use of steam – watch for stretching of units through pressing.

Care taken in each of these cases will decrease blood pressure and frustration. You will feel in charge!

Among the best investments you can make are a quarter-inch presser foot for your machine, an accurate ruler, and a critical eye.

Threadles

A Threadle is a piece of folded fabric that is used when machine sewing off and onto a project. Using a Threadle helps to avoid fabric being caught in the feed dogs; eliminate having to cut off threads for a neat finish; prevent uncut threads from showing through a quilt top; and save thread.

To make a Threadle, fold a 2" x 3" piece of fabric in half lengthwise and insert it under the presser foot at the start of sewing. Run the machine a little between the Threadle and your sewing. Once you've taken three or four stitches, snip the Threadle off but keep it close at hand. When finishing your seam, sew from your piece back onto the Threadle. Between sewing, leave the Threadle under the foot of your machine with the needle in the down position.

(1) A Threadle deeper than 1" when folded will waste rather than save thread. The Threadle can be as long as you wish.

(2) Don't be scared to run empty stitches between the Threadle and your fabric. The thread will twist neatly and make an easier cut.

When you have to start sewing in the middle of an already partially sewn line, you can still use the Threadle. Turn the fabric crosswise of the needle, and sew from the Threadle to the stitched line. Leave the needle in the down position, turn the fabric 90°, and continue the seam as required. Leave the needle in the down position, turn and sew off the side of the fabric back onto a Threadle. This keeps your work very neat. If you want to press seams open, just flick the stitches out of the way.

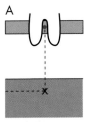

From Threadle onto fabric

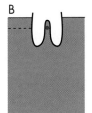

Needle down

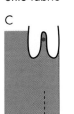

Turn and sew

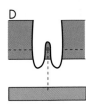

Needle down, turn and sew onto Threadle

Chain Sewing

When sewing multiple units, run your machine a few stitches between pieces, letting the thread twist and spread between the units. Do not cut too closely or the first few stitches will unravel from the edge.

Pieced Borders

Borders are often one of the most neglected parts of a quilt. After all the cutting and piecing, the top has taken such a lot of work that all you want to do is get the borders on and be finished. The thought of more work piecing a border is depressing.

Here's where you can use the bonus triangles you saved from piecing the quilt top. Play with the bonus units – double them up (combine two rows as in KOWHAI). Try "spacers" (unpieced units) between bonus units so there is not so much piecing. The combinations are endless, allowing you to be more innovative than you thought possible.

Make the space between the quilt top and the binding work for you. Ask yourself – could the quilt benefit from a small inner border, then a pieced border before the final, wider unpieced section? Give your imagination full rein! The end product will be worth it. A well-balanced border adds that final touch and is another chance to individualize and enhance your magical quilt!

A small inner border can brighten or define the central elements, giving the quilt a better dimension. Always "audition" and manipulate the inner border until you feel the balance is good. With borders, even a quarter-inch larger or smaller can make a vast difference in the feel of the quilt.

The type of border you use should reflect the aesthetic quality of the quilt's main area. A successful method is using a unit that is already in the quilt's pieced blocks as in OAKLANDS (pg. 92), VINTAGE NELSON (pg. 53), and PIGEON VALLEY (pg. 77).

Borders

Make sure you square the ends of your border strips using your ruler. Also make certain that all corners of the quilt top are squared.

Cut the side borders together and do the same with the top and bottom borders. I prefer to use a metal builders' retracting tape for practically everything to do with measuring quilt tops, batting, backing, borders, etc. The metal doesn't stretch and is more accurate than a cloth measuring tape. It also retracts neatly. You can find one at the nearest hardware or building supply store.

For the projects in this book, exact border length cutting instructions are given. It pays, however, to always check by taking your own measurements before cutting.

Fold the borders and the quilt top to mark the halfway and quarter points. Pin together at these points, and especially at both ends, with an extra pin to secure across the width of the border at either end. This will keep your border fabric square with the quilt top. Multi-pin between pins, allowing for any easing of fabric evenly along the length of the seam.

As you attach each border piece, press them back carefully, pressing toward the outer edge, not along the length of the fabric. Many quilters put borders on each side first, then add the last borders to the top and bottom. Remember, these top and bottom borders are measured from the full width of the top and both side borders, so remember to cut them wide enough. If you are short of fabric, cut squares of a complementary fabric for each corner. Carefully square the corners when you have finished attaching the last border.

Mitering Borders

When mitering borders, fabric for the borders must be cut the full length and width of the finished quilt. Follow the basic principles above and in "Cutting" (pg. 31).

Put a pencil mark on your quilt top in each corner, ¼" down from the top and ¼" in from the side. This one pencil mark will be where you start and finish sewing the borders onto the quilt. The ends will remain unsewn at this stage and will need to be folded back to avoid being caught in the next line of stitching.

¼" STOP

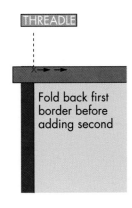
THREADLE

Fold back first border before adding second

Follow the basic instructions already given in "Borders," especially for folding and pinning together at the quarter and halfway marks. When you have attached the first side, fold the surplus fabric back and pin it out of the way.

Once you have pinned the second border piece in place, ready to sew, insert a pin through the border fabric directly into the mark in the corner ¼" from both edges. This should be on the spot where the last row of stitching stopped.

Using your Threadle, sew onto the border fabric, making sure the needle goes down into the ¼" mark. With needle down, turn the fabric and sew a seam to the next end ¼" mark. Leave the needle in the down position, turn the fabric sideways, and sew off the quilt onto the Threadle. Attach the last two borders in the same manner.

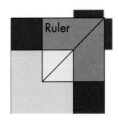
Ruler

With all borders attached, lay the quilt on a flat surface, right side up. Unfold the spare fabric and lay each piece flat and square, one on top of the other. Using the square edge of your ruler, trim off any excess. Be extremely careful!

With the bottom section of the border laying flat, fold the top section under itself at a 45°

fold
lay quilt flat

angle as illustrated. Adjust the fold until it is perfect. You should see a clear fold starting from the inside corner to matching edges at the outer corner.

Masking Tape
Fold Line

Finger press the folded edge then anchor the mitered corner with masking tape as shown.

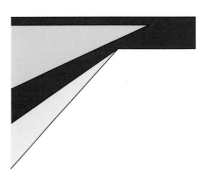

Fold right sides together so the seam lines of the borders match. The end of both seams should meet. Make sure that nothing is bending back on itself and that inside layers are flat to avoid "catching."

The masking tape will fold in half right on the edge of the 45° angle, leaving a good edge to sew on. You can help this a little by using your fingernail to give a sharp line, or marking with a fine pencil or a sliver of soap.

Stitch on the line, but be careful not to get adhesive from the masking tape onto the needle. Turn right side out and check the seam by removing the masking tape.

If you are a little nervous doing this method the first time, use a larger stitch till you've had time to check, then go back and do a normal row of sewing. Once you are pleased with the result, remove the masking tape. Trim off excess fabric to a ¼" seam allowance and press the seams open.

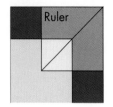

The last step is checking to be sure the corners are square and the diagonal line of your ruler matches the miter.

Binding

It would be a shame to complete a beautiful quilt and then hurry through the binding.

Trim backing and batting to within ¼" of the edge of the quilt top. Cut binding fabric into 2½" strips and stitch them together to the required length plus 8"–10" extra. Fold the binding in half, right side out.

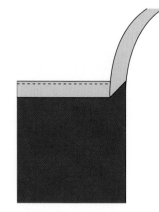

Before you start sewing the binding, open and fold the edge over to form a 45° angle as shown, with the cut edge matching the edge of the quilt top.

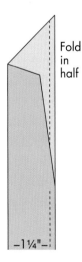

Sew the first 4" as a single layer. Pull the fabric out from under the needle, fold the binding back in half and start sewing where you left off. This will leave a flap to accommodate the finished end of the binding.

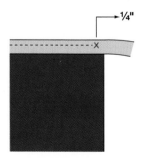

Begin attaching your binding about two-thirds of the way down the right side. When you reach the first corner, sew to within a quarter-inch of the edge.

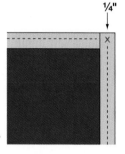

With the needle in the down position, turn the quilt so it is ready to be sewn down the next side. Backstitch off the edge of the quilt, leaving enough room to be able to fold the binding as shown.

When the binding is in the position shown, make sure the top of the fold is level with the edge of the quilt. Look at the underneath portion of the fold to make sure both layers of the fold are even on the top left side. Accurate folding at this stage gives a very neatly mitered corner when the binding is folded to the back.

Start sewing again (the ¼" seam should meet at the point where you stopped in the previous row). Repeat the miter for each corner. To finish, insert the end of the binding into the bias fold and finish stitching.

To complete the binding, fold it to the back of the quilt, just enough to cover the stitch line, and hand stitch it down. Use cotton thread that matches the binding. Just catch the edge and take the thread straight down at the same point. Let the needle travel along under the fabric to come out where you take the next tiny stitch. You may need to trim back the corners a little but always keep the binding "full." At the corners, the back of the binding folds in the opposite direction to the front. This makes a neatly mitered corner on the back of the quilt as well. Put a couple of stitches into the miter to hold it in place, especially if you are using flannel.

Problem Solvers

Pre-washing

• First, stop the laundry! I prefer to wash (cold water, no detergent) all fabrics because of variations in the rates of shrinkage and the possibility of "bleeding." Cut the corner off each selvage edge to help check excessive fraying during washing.

• Don't use sheets of fabric softener – they can cause grease spots.

Cutting

• When making scrap quilts, you can save fabric and time by cutting a strip of the widest width you'll need. For instance, if the cutting chart says you will need 2½" squares AND 2⅞" squares from the same fabric, cut the wider width first. You can then get both sizes from one strip and save a lot of waste!

• Make one block first before cutting the rest of the quilt. This acts as a good check that the directions are accurate, that you have followed them accurately, and that the first block gives the result you want. If you want to change one of the fabrics, it is easy to do at this stage.

• Bulk cutting – Once you've cut and sewn your first block and are happy with it, then you can bulk cut. Write separate cutting notes for each fabric (self-sticking note pads are great), and post only that cutting instruction in front of you. With the next fabric, use another note. When you're getting tired and should have stopped ages ago, it's just too easy to read the wrong line.

• If you are using any of the block fabrics for borders, cut the lengths needed for both inner and outer borders before proceeding with general cutting for the blocks. Label and put them aside. Do the same for the fabric to be used for binding.

Once the quilt is finished, however, another fabric or fabrics may prove a better choice for the binding. Let the quilt tell you. The fabric you've saved for the binding won't be wasted, I'm sure!

• When cutting binding, I normally use 2½" strips. Fold and iron the strips in half with wrong sides together. Wrap them around a cardboard tube and store, ready for use.

• When cutting borders, measure down and across the center of your quilt top as well as the outside edges. Cut the borders to the nearest "center" measurement. This will ensure that the borders don't "wave."

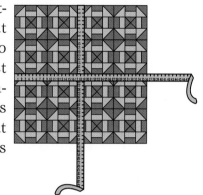

If there is a variation between the center and side measurements, make small adjustments in several of the quilt top's side seams rather than one or two larger adjustments. If you've ever seen a lovely quilt spoiled by wavy borders, the reason could be that the borders were made to fit the top, rather than the top made to fit the borders. Make sense? Hope so!

Settling into temporary quarters in an ancient ruin, Squirty and Squiffy measure for a decorative wallpaper border.

Sewing

• When putting two pieces together in preparing to sew, if they don't quite match, stop and measure. Trim if necessary, or re-cut. Small differences become far greater as they extend out into the block. Check the accuracy of your cutting frequently.

• It can help to lay out the blocks you intend to sew on flat pieces of cardboard or trays. Chain sewing two blocks at a time is not difficult. Separate the blocks by having one set on each side of the machine. Once the second piece is under the needle, remove the first piece and put it back where it came from. This creates a continuous rhythm and the flow is surprisingly easy to master.

• When one fabric has stretched slightly more than another, place the stretchy piece on the bottom when sewing. The feed dogs will usually take up the surplus.

• Points not matching? Unpick up to an inch on either side of the points. Look to see if the raw edges are meeting. Move the offending piece backward or forward (usually the pointed piece needs to be moved back a little) and this will be enough to correct the fault.

• After unpicking, spray the pieces with water or spray starch, then press. Fabric gets "tired" with too much handling. Spraying and pressing helps it sew up again like new!

Pressing

• Finger press where possible during block construction and leave ironing till the block is finished. Don't be too heavy handed and preferably don't use steam, or you could distort the block. When units, especially small ones, are consistently giving you a problem even when you know your cutting and sewing are accurate, pressing could be the cause.

• Pin a large safety pin near the tip of your ironing board cover and a second toward the rear of the board. Fold your binding strip in

half and thread it through the pins. The pins will help hold the strip in place while you iron.

• To avoid fabric distortion, iron in the direction of the grain when possible.

• Press sewn seams flat (just as they've been sewn) before pressing the unit open. This gives a "sharper" flatter seam line.

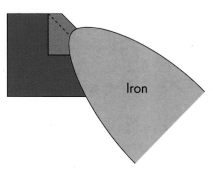

• Just slide the iron between the units gently, easing the triangle into place.

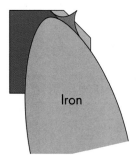

• Within the first one or two blocks, decide which way you will need to press seam allowances for ease in joining to the next block. In order to gain the best effect in the quilting, some designs will need to ignore the rule of pressing to the dark. Considering all of this before making too many blocks will prevent the grief of finding that the quilting would have looked better if the seam lines had gone the other way.

Quilting

• Trace or draw your quilting design on paper and cut several layers of paper the same size. To repeat the pattern, use an unthreaded jeans needle and stitch through all layers. To mark the design through the holes in the paper, use cornstarch on a cotton ball for dark fabrics or cinnamon for light fabrics. If you prefer, you can then go over the design with a silver or fine, hard pencil.

• Knots in your quilting thread? Run your thumbnail on the knot in the opposite direction, or put the needle inside the loop and pull in the opposite direction.

• When threading a quilting needle, cut the thread on an angle, wet the thread and wet the eye of the needle. Hold the thread in your left hand and move the needle onto the thread. It works!

• Make quilting templates from adhesive shelf paper. They can be placed and moved many times before needing to be replaced.

• Whether hand or pin basting, use a spoon to help guide the needle or safety pin through the layers of fabric and batting. Your fingernails will appreciate it.

• When going from one point to another to quilt, run the needle between the fabric layers as far as you can, then push the needle point halfway up through the fabric. Grasping the point, swivel the needle so that the head is pointing in the direction you want to go – push the head through the fabric layers beneath the surface and swivel again. Keep traveling like this until you reach the point you want to start quilting again. Just be careful not to pull the connecting thread too tight or it will pucker your work. And don't forget your thimble!

General

• Keep a note of your bed sizes handy to save measuring each time.

• To find the width of a square set on point, multiply by 1.414. For example, a 10" square set on point will measure 14.14" across. Convert the measurement to the nearest fraction.

• If you know the measurement of the long side of a triangle and want to find out what size square is needed to cut two triangles, multiply by .707.

• A retractable metal tape of the type used by builders is extremely accurate and doesn't stretch as do fabric tapes. Metal tapes extend the full length of a quilt and are ideal for measuring borders. Once extended, they self-lock.

Make a Statement

Labels
Labels are another chance to make your quilt say something! If you make a lot of quilts, find your own theme and turn that theme into a label. You may love making house blocks so you could make your labels in the form of a house – just write your name/date/place and the name of the quilt within that block and it becomes your signature. Apples, pigs, specific flowers – whatever your fancy, use it, but make it YOURS!

Jeanette is a part-time pilot and uses a cute label with four propellers on her quilts. Another of the UnderCover Girls always puts an animal fabric (usually very subtle) somewhere in her quilts. If she can't use it on the front, she puts it on the back or as part of the label. She began the practice when her grandson saw an elephant in her first quilt and thereafter asked where the animal was.

Backings
Further statements can be made by creating a pieced back. Use leftover fabrics or blocks from the front of the quilt, add one or two more if necessary, and have fun placing and piecing a unique back. Make a comment with the back of your quilt so that when you turn it over, there's a surprise, rather like an exclamation mark! TASMAN BAY uses fabric bought for but not used in the top and BERRIED TREASURES uses a pair of coordinated sheets, dyed and pieced for good effect.

Yardage Calculation Chart

Working on a basis of 42" wide fabric, multiply the number of strips by the strip depth.

Color	Unit	1st cut	2nd cut	No. units to block/blocks to quilt	No. in 42" fabric width	No. of strips	x	Strip depth	= Yardage (add 5%)	Total
Sample Red	Tri-2	2½"	2½"	4x20 = 80	16	5		2½"	12½"	14"

Number of Squares That Can Be Cut from a 42" Fabric Width

Size	Yield	Size	Yield	Size	Yield	Size	Yield
1½"	28	1¾"	24	2"	21	2¼"	18
2½"	16	2¾"	15	3"	14	3¼"	12
3½"	12	3¾"	11	4"	10	4¼"	9
4½"	9	4¾"	8	5"	8	5¼"	8
5½"	7	5¾"	7	6"	7	6¼"	6

- Count the number of units in each block and multiply by the number of blocks. For example, 4 units to a block, 30 blocks in the quilt, would require 4 x 30 = 120 units to cut.

- Use the narrowest measurement for the first cut. For example, if you need 2½" x 5" pieces, cut 2½" strips across the width of the fabric. Then cut the strips into 5" lengths. You will get eight cuts of 5" from the 42" width of the fabric.

- Count the number of units required (120) by the number of units yielded across the strip (8). Divide 8 into 120 and you will find you need 15–2½" strips.

$$120 \div 8 = 15$$

- To find the amount of fabric needed, multiply 15 (the number of strips needed) by 2½" (the depth of each cut for the strips).

$$15 \times 2½" = 37½"$$

You will need 37½" of fabric. Always allow a little extra fabric for glitches and shrinkage – usually 5 percent will cover both.

- Add borders to the above fabric calculations. Calculate the borders by using the full length of the fabric. Cut and reserve the border fabric by labeling and putting it aside. Use the remainder for piecing in the body of the quilt. If you intend to use self-binding, follow the same procedure as for borders.

Projects

BERRIED TREASURES
(Pieced and hand quilted by Alison Crawford)

These large 18" blocks suited a king-sized quilt and did not look out of place. On a quilt for a smaller bed, 12" blocks would look better (see LIVE IN HOPE – 12" blocks, pg. 40). Alison designed leaves and berries to hand quilt on the light areas of each block.

Uncovering Traditional Quilts – Joyce Jones

BERRIED TREASURES

Finished size:	98" x 116"
Finished block size:	18"
Number of blocks:	20 (4 x 5)

Fabric Required

Dark	3¼ yards
Light	3¼ yards
Small print	2 yards
Medium	1½ yards
Floral	4¾ yards

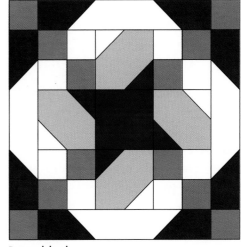

Basic block

Finished units required for each block

      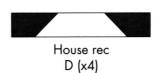

Center	4-Patch	Sq-2	House rec	Squares	Squiffy
A (x1)	B (x4)	C (x4)	D (x4)	E (x4)	F

Cutting instructions are for the entire quilt.

Unit	Fabric	Strips	1st cut	2nd cut	No.	Unit assembly
A	Medium	3	5"	5"	20	
B	Small print	12	2¾"	2¾"	160	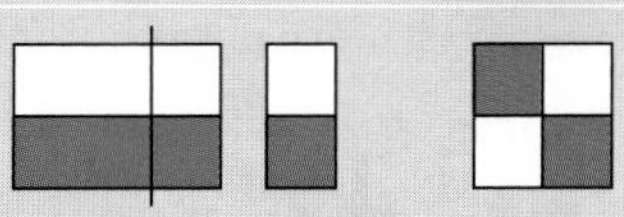
	Light	12	2¾"	2¾"	160	

• *Sew strips together then cut into 2¾" units.*

C	Floral	10	5"	5"	80	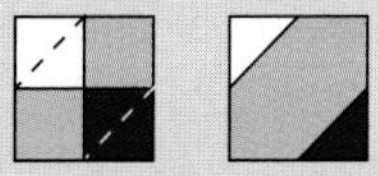
	Light	6	2¾"	2¾"	80	
	Medium	6	2¾"	2¾"	80	

• *Squiffy one light and one medium square to opposite corners of a floral square.*

D	Dark	20	2¾"	5"	160	
	Light	20	2¾"	9½"	80	

E	Small print	6	2¾"	2¾"	80	

• *Attach E squares to each end of half of the D units.*

F	Floral	3	2"	2"	48	

• *This floral is Squiffied onto the corners of some finished blocks (see Corner Squiffies, next page).*

Block Construction

Sew the center section together in rows of three. Then sew the three rows together to form the central part of the block. Attach House Recs to two sides of the central block.

Add squares to each end of two House Recs and attach them to the top and bottom of the block.

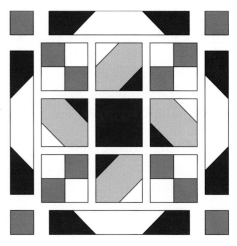

Corner Squiffies

Study the quilt and you will see that a floral Squiffy was added to the completed blocks. It was added only in the central section and not the outer edges, providing extra sparkle to what would have finished as a plain square. You have a choice at this stage whether to add Squiffies or not.

Lay the blocks out in rows of 4 x 5 then pin a 2" square of floral to the central corner – you will need 48. Squiffy the squares to these corners before joining the blocks together. Doing it this way gives the impression they are floating. Press these last seams open to help achieve accuracy.

4 corner blocks - Add 1, 2" floral Squiffy to one corner of each block.

10 side blocks - Add 2, 2" floral Squiffies to the corners of one edge of each block.

6 center blocks - Add 4, 2" floral Squiffies to the corners of each block.

Multiple Borders

The pieced border extends the blocks, giving added dimension to the quilt. Another row of dark before the final borders adds to the "floating" effect. The small red border brings the focus back to the red stars in the body of the quilt.

Fabric	Strips	1st cut	2nd cut	No.		Unit
First Border						
Dark	5	2¾"	16¼"	10		
Dark	4	2¾"	17⅜"	8		
Small print	2	2¾"	2¾"	18		

Assemble two side pieced border strips as follows:

17⅜" + Square (Sq) + 16¼" + Sq + 16¼" + Sq + 16¼" + Sq + 17⅜"
(start and finish with the longer strip) Attach to the sides of the quilt top.

Assemble two top and bottom pieced border strips and attach as follows:

Sq + 17⅜" + Sq + 16¼" + Sq + 16¼" + Sq + 17⅜" + Sq
(start and finish with a longer strip plus a square at either end)

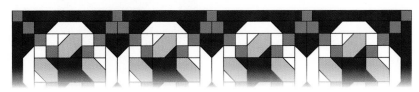

Fabric	Strips	1st cut	2nd cut	
Second border				
Dark	2	2¾"	95"	Add to each side.
Dark	2	2¾"	81½"	Add to top and bottom.
Third border				
Small print	2	1"	99½"	Add to each side.
Small print	2	1"	82½"	Add to top and bottom.
Fourth border				
Medium	2	1½"	100½"	Add to each side.
Medium	2	1½"	84½"	Add to top and bottom.
Final border				
Floral	2	7½"	102½"	Add to each side.
Floral	2	7½"	98½"	Add to top and bottom.
Binding				
Floral	12	2½"	450"	(refer to Binding, pg. 30)

BERRIED TREASURES

Design Double Take

LIVE IN HOPE

(Pieced by Carolyn McKay;
machine quilted by Bev Dyke)
Finished size: 59" x 73"
Finished block size: 12"
Number of blocks: 20 (4 x 5)

Basic block

This is a lovely scrap plaid version of BERRIED TREASURES, but notice that the values have been changed. Sashing with connector stars adds to the interest. Carolyn felt happy with the two small borders and scrap binding. The only coordinated fabrics are the muslin and the two fabrics used for outer sashing and borders.

BISHOPDALE
(Pieced and machine quilted by Betty Gilbert)

The center square and corners in this quilt are of medium value, with dark units around the center. Scraps of decorator fabrics contrasted with a muslin background and border provide a crisp, clean look. Betty used swags and cross-hatch quilting in the border and multi-scrap binding. It is extremely economical! Make this quilt block by block. You can make decisions on color choices as you build up to the number of blocks needed.

BISHOPDALE

Finished size:	69" x 94"
Finished block size:	9"
Number of blocks:	39 (set on point)

Fabric Required

Muslin . . . . 6½ yards
Scraps (minimum per block)
    Medium . . . . 4" x 20"
    Dark . . . . 4" x 20"

Basic block

Finished units required for each block

Center	Tri-2	Rec-1R	Rec-1R
A (x1)	B (x4)	C (x4)	D (x4)

The amount of scrap required to make each block is shown in parentheses and is rounded to the nearest inch. The muslin cutting instructions are for the whole quilt.

Unit	Fabric	Strips	1ˢᵗ cut	2ⁿᵈ cut	No.	Unit assembly
A	Medium	scrap (4"x4")	3½"	3½"	1	
B	Muslin	10	3⅞"	3⅞"	78	
	Dark	scrap (4"x9")	3⅞"	3⅞"	2	
C	Muslin	20	2"	3½"	156	
	Dark	scrap (3"x9")	2"	2"	4	
D	Medium	scrap (3"x15")	2"	3½"	4	
	Muslin	10	2"	2"	156	

• *Join Units C, B, and D.*

Block Construction

Using the Start-a-Seam method, add one of the C, B, and D units to Unit A as shown. Add successive rounds as illustrated. Finish the original seam, starting at the outer edge and join with the first seam line.

Side Setting Units

Remove selvages and straighten the first cutting edge using your cutting board as a guide. Cut strips, then cut the first 45° angle at the measurement given. Turn the remaining fabric and repeat the process. Two X units take 35" and two Y units take 31½". Each 9½" strip yields two units.

BISHOPDALE

Unit assembly

Unit	Fabric	Strips	1st cut	2nd cut	No.
X	Muslin	2	9½"	22¼"	4
Y	Muslin	8	9½"	20½"	16

(Note the placement of the X and Y units in the Quilt assembly diagram, pg. 44)

Scrap Finishing Units

	Muslin	4	2"	9½"	16
	Medium lt.	2	2"	3½"	16

Sew to the 16 Y side setting units (9½" x 20½") as illustrated. If you choose not to use the scrap corner units, simply cut all 20 side setting pieces 9½" x 22¼".

Corners

	Muslin		12"	12"	2

Cut the two 12" squares into four half-triangles. To achieve the angles needed for the four corners, trim 3½" off the right hand corner of each triangle as shown.

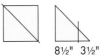

8½" 3½"

Quilt Assembly

Lay the blocks in a diagonal set. Add the completed Y units to each of the rows as shown, finally adding the X and corner pieces as in the illustration.

For ease of construction, assemble the quilt top in five parts – A, B, C, D and E.

Join A and B. Join C and D. The E row connects both sections.

Spray starch bias edges on X and Y units to prevent stretching while handling. If preferred, stitch each bias edge with strong cotton thread, leaving loose ends. If stretching has occurred, pull on the thread to ease the edge back into shape before adding binding.

Quilting

Large areas of plain muslin border enabled a lovely deep swag to be set into cross-hatching.

Binding

Fabric	1st cut	2nd cut
Mixed scrap	2½"	340"

(refer to Binding, pg. 30)

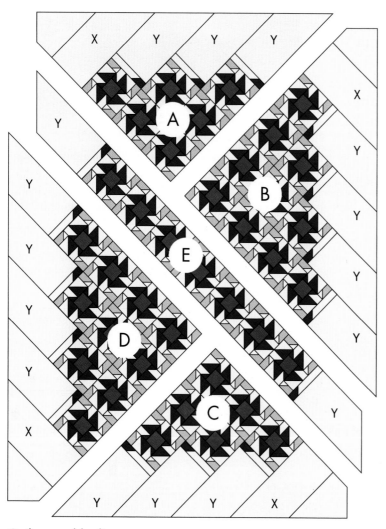

Quilt assembly diagram

Design Double Take

KATH'S REEL

(Pieced by Kath Beresford;
machine quilted by Bev Dyke)

Finished size: 60" x 87"
Finished block size: 12"
Number of blocks: 24 (4 x 6)

Basic block

KATH'S REEL uses the same basic block design as does BISHOPDALE, but with a more casual result. Setting the blocks straight rather than on point and using lots of scraps give this design its appeal. Because the colors are so low in contrast, the black sashing and outer strip give more definition and clarity to the colors. The black you see is actually the dull side of black chintz. Note the use of controlled squares in the sashing and borders.

CHILD'S PLAY
(Pieced and machine quilted by Marion Dixon)

This beautifully simple quilt was made to look like a child's board game. You could also use "kiddie" prints to make it an "I Spy." Use the same value dark fabrics in units C and D, but piece them separately for more variety. The color change in the first inner border came from the use of one color graded fabric. Make the A units a mixture of scraps for each of the eight blocks. In the quilt shown, the four center Nine-patch blocks are lighter than the four corners. You choose!

CHILD'S PLAY

Finished size: 39" square
Finished block size: 6"
Number of blocks: 25 (5 x 5)

Fabric Required

Multi light, Medium, and Dark scraps

1st border . . . . ⅓ yard
2nd border . . . . ¼ yard
3rd border . . . . ⅓ yard
Binding . . . . ⅓ yard

Quilt design

Finished units required for this quilt

A (x8)   B (x8)   C (x8)   D (x1)   E (x12)   F (x8)   G (x4)
                           Center

Unit	Fabric	1st cut	2nd cut	Pieces	Unit assembly
A	Lights (mixed)	2½"	2½"	36	
	Darks & mediums (mixed)	2½"	2½"	36	
• *Assemble Nine-patch units in various ways.*					
B	Light	6½"	6½"	8	
	Dark	2½"	2½"	16	
C	Dark	2½"	6½"	16	
	Lights (mixed)	2½"	2½"	24	
D	Dark	2½"	2½"	5	
	Light	2½"	2½"	4	
• *Assemble Nine-patch unit as shown.*					

Quilt Assembly

Sew the units together in rows as shown.

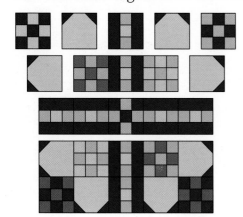

CHILD'S PLAY

First border

Unit assembly

Unit	Fabric	1st cut	2nd cut	No.
E	Light	2½"	6½"	12
	Dark	2½"	2½"	24
F	Light	2½"	6½"	8
G	Medium	2½"	2½"	4

First Border Construction

Sew units E and F in two rows as shown then attach to each side of the quilt.

Sew units E and F in two rows as shown, with added corners (Unit G). Attach to the top and bottom of the quilt.

Second Border

	Bright	1"	34½"	2	Add to each side.
	Bright	1"	35½"	2	Add to top and bottom.

Outer Border

	Dark	2½"	35½"	4	Add one to each of two sides of the quilt top.

Corners (Make as for Square-in-a-Square units, pg. 15)

	Bright	2½"	2½"	4
	Dark	1½"	1½"	16

Add a corner to each end of two outer border strips. Attach them to top and bottom.

Binding

	Dark	2½"	168"		(refer to Binding, pg. 30)

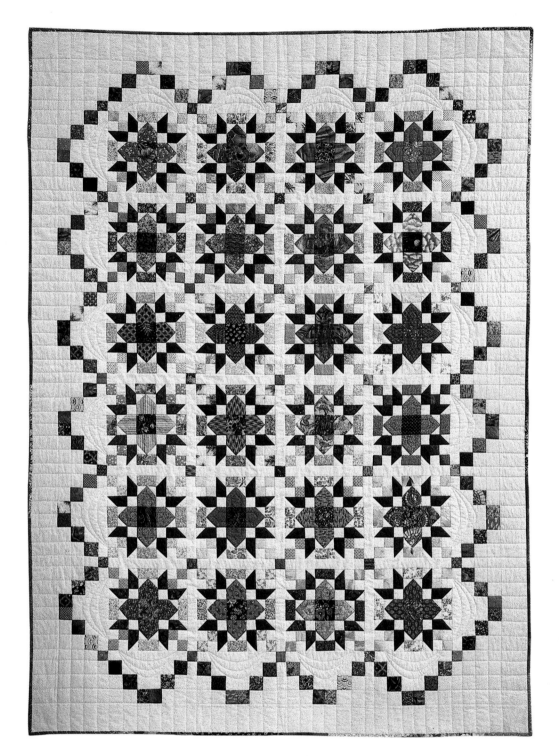

D'URVILLE
(Pieced by Pat Buchanan; machine quilted by Bev Dyke)

Pulling the fabrics together for one block, cutting and sewing as you go, leaves room for change and variety. The instructions in this project are for one block. For a more interesting result, change the values slightly as you progress. Pat used compatible print fabrics for the centers and Goose's End units. She also used a mixture of very dark solid blues for the Rec-1L and Rec-1R units (F and G), plus medium lights for the Four-patches and rectangles.

D'
U
r
v
i
l
l
e

D'URVILLE

Finished size:	76" x 103"
Finished block size:	12"
Number of blocks:	24 (4 x 6)

Fabric Required

Muslin . . . . 5½ yards
Binding . . . . ¾ yards
Scraps (minimum per block)
    Medium . . . . 8" square
    Dark . . . . 8" square
    Focal print . . . . 8" square

Basic block

Finished units required for each block

Center A (x1)	4-Patch B (x4)	Goose's End C (x4)	Rec D (x4)	Rec-1L E (x4)	Rec-1R F (x4)	Squares G (x4)

The amount of scrap required to make each block is shown in parentheses.
Muslin cutting instructions are for the whole quilt.

Unit	Fabric	Size/Strips	1ˢᵗ cut	2ⁿᵈ cut	No.	Unit assembly
A	Focal print	(3½" sq.)	3½"	3½"	1	
B	Muslin	10	2"	2"	8 (x24)	
	Medium	(2" x 16")	2"	2"	8	

• *Join strips then cut into 2" units. Join two units to make 4-patch.*

C	Focal print	(3½" x 15")	3½"	3½"	4	
	Muslin	10	2"	2"	8 (x24)	

• *Squiffy the muslin squares as shown, noting that they should overlap as in a Flying Geese unit.*

D	Medium	(2" x 15")	2"	3½"	4	

• *Add to the top of unit C.*

E	Dark	(2" x 15")	2"	3½"	4	
	Muslin	5	2"	2"	4 (x24)	

• *Squiffy the muslin squares to form Rec-1Ls.*

Unit	Fabric	Size or Strip	1ˢᵗ cut	2ⁿᵈ cut	No.	Unit assembly
F	Muslin	5	2"	2"	4 (x24)	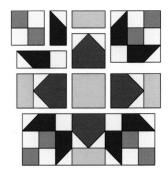
	Dark	(2" x 15")	2"	3½"	4	

• *Squiffy the muslin squares to form Rec-1Rs.*

| G | Muslin | 5 | 2" | 2" | 4 (x24) | |

Block Assembly

Assemble block as shown, connecting units in three rows, then join-ing rows together.

Sashing

Fabric	Strips	1ˢᵗ cut	2ⁿᵈ cut	No.
Muslin	20	2"	12½"	58

Connector Squares

Fabric		1ˢᵗ cut	2ⁿᵈ cut	No.
Scraps		2"	2"	35

Quilt Top Assembly

Set blocks 4 x 6 – attach sashing strips to ver-tical sides as shown.

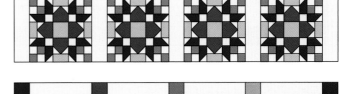

Join connector squares to horizontal sash-ing as shown and attach to top, bottom, and between rows.

Outer Pieced Borders

The sashing between blocks in the quilt top was cut 2". The units being used for the pieced border are based on 2½" cuts. This has been taken into account in the cutting instructions, but still take care when constructing the rows.

Pieced Border Assembly

All muslin border pieces can be cut from 13–2½" strips of muslin.

Row 1

Fabric	1ˢᵗ cut	2ⁿᵈ cut	No.
Muslin	2½"	2"	24
Muslin	2½"	8½"	20
Scrap	2½"	2½"	40

Set out and sew as below, starting and finishing with 2½" x 2" muslin. Make two strips for the sides using six 2½" x 8½" muslin strips. Repeat, using four muslin strips for the top and bottom sections. Do not attach to the quilt at this stage.

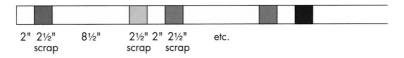

2" 2½"   8½"   2½" 2" 2½"   etc.
    scrap   scrap scrap

D'Urville

Fabric	1st cut	2nd cut	No.
Row 2			
Muslin	2½"	4"	8
Muslin	2½"	4½"	20
Muslin	2½"	6"	16
Scrap	2½"	2½"	40

Arrange and sew as below, starting and finishing with a 4" rectangle. Make two strips for the sides using 12 scrap squares. Make two strips for the top and bottom using 8 scrap squares.

D'URVILLE

4" 2½" 4½" 2½" 6" 2½" etc.
     scrap   scrap   scrap

Fabric	1st cut	2nd cut	No.
Row 3			
Muslin	2½"	6"	8
Muslin	2½"	10"	16
Scrap	2½"	2½"	40

Arrange and sew as below, starting and finishing with 6" muslin strips. Make two strips for the sides using six 10" muslin strips. Make two strips for the top and bottom using four, 10" muslin strips.

6" 2½" 2½" 10" 2½" 2½" 10" etc.
    scrap scrap   scrap scrap

Border Construction

Sew the three rows together as shown.

Attach the two longer units to the sides.

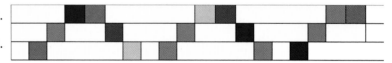

Pieced Border Corners

Fabric	1st cut	2nd cut	No.
Muslin	6½"	6½"	4

Sew a corner square to each end of the top and bottom pieced borders before attaching.

Outer Border

Fabric	1st cut	2nd cut	No.	
Muslin	4½"	95"	2	Sew to sides.
Muslin	4½"	77"	2	Sew to top and bottom.

To avoid piecing borders, you may prefer to cut these borders on the length of the fabric.

Binding

Fabric	1st cut	2nd cut	
Muslin	2½"	370"	(refer to section on
or mixed scrap			Binding, pg. 30)

Design Double Take

Vintage Nelson

(Pieced and hand quilted by Lois Zachariassen)

Finished size:	84" x 96"
Finished block size:	12"
Number of blocks:	30 (5 x 6)

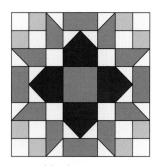

Basic block

It is amazing how different the same block can appear when used in a different way. Vintage Nelson uses two variations of the block used in D'Urville. Study the blocks so you understand the positive and negative placement of color values within them. There are 30 blocks, 15 each of two variations. The Goose's End units in the quilt are a strong inner border design element.

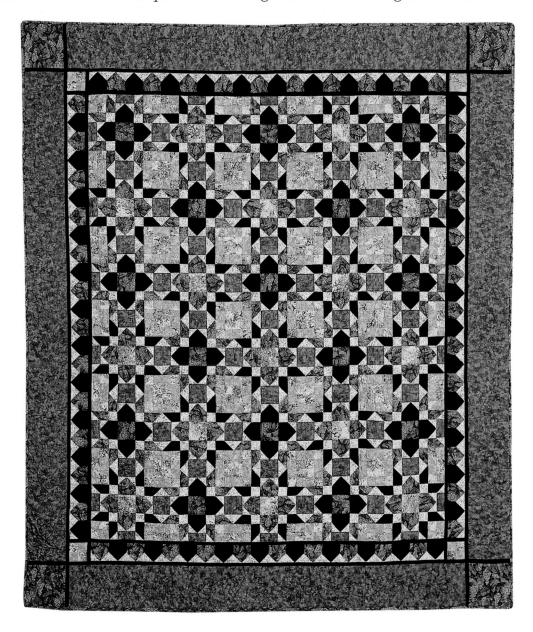

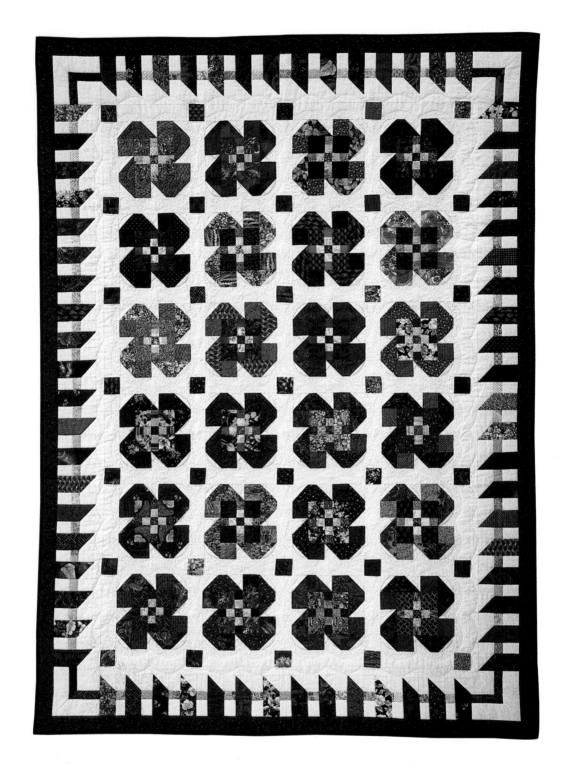

FENCED IN
(Pieced by Joyce Jones; machine quilted by Bev Dyke)

The block used for FENCED IN was designed for FLANNEL FLOWERS (pg. 63) where it worked with soft flannels as a lap quilt. The more I looked at the block, the more I realized how suitable the pattern would be for a totally scrap quilt. Use different fabrics for units D and E, but it is important that they have similar values or the block's appearance will change.

FENCED IN

Finished size: 62" x 84"
Finished block size: 9"
Number of blocks: 24 (4 x 6)

Fabric Required

Muslin . . . . 3½ yards
Dark . . . . 1¼ yards
  (for border and binding)
Scraps (minimum per block)
    Medium . . . . 3" square
    Dark #1 . . . . 12" square
    Dark #2 . . . . 6" square
    Floral . . . . 6" square

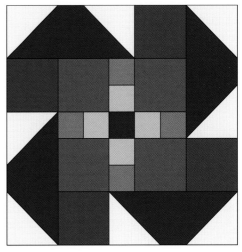

Basic block

Finished units required for each block

A (x4)	Square B (x1)	Square C (x4)	House Rec D (x4)	Square E (x4)

Unit	Fabric	1ˢᵗ cut	2ⁿᵈ cut	No.	Unit assembly
Block center					
A	Light	1½"	1½"	4	
	Medium	1½"	1½"	4	

• *Sew strips together then cut into 1½" units.*

B	Dark #1	1½"	1½"	1	

• *Attach a B square between two A units as shown.*

C	Floral	2½"	2½"	4	

• *Assemble block center as shown.*

Unit	Fabric	1st cut	2nd cut	No.	Unit assembly
D	Dark #1	2½"	5½"	4	
	Muslin	2½"	2½"	8	
E	Dark #2	2½"	2½"	4	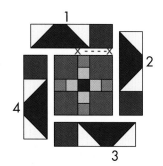

- *Add an E unit to the right side of a D unit as shown.*

 Squares can be made of different darks but keep the values similar. Go too light or dark and the whole block changes, and not for the best!

Block Construction

Using the Start-a-Seam method, assemble blocks as shown.

Sashing

Fabric	Strips	1st cut	2nd cut	No.
Muslin	15	2½"	9½"	58

Attach vertical sashing as shown and connect blocks. Make five rows of four blocks each.

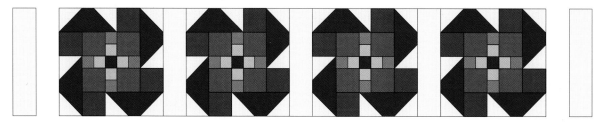

Connector Squares

Floral scraps	2	2½"	2½"	30

Assemble connector squares and sashing as shown. Attach to top, bottom, and between each row of blocks.

Picket Fence Border

Use any leftovers from cutting the 1½" centers and stitch them together just "as they come" to form railings.

Fabric	1st cut	2nd cut	No.	Unit assembly
Muslin	2½"	68½"	2	

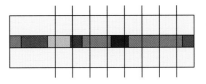

Sew a 2½" strip of muslin on each side of the scrap strip and cut into 64–2" segments for the railings. I took no notice of the various piecing seams in the railings and was pleased with the effect, but you may wish to avoid them.

Pickets

Dark	2½"	5½"	68	
Muslin	2½"	2½"	68	

Squiffy Rec-1Rs to form the pickets.

Alternate picket units with railing units as shown.

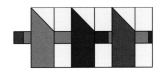

Pieced borders present some interesting challenges in making the units fit the edges of the quilt. In order to make the whole thing "work," it may be necessary to shave off a little extra fabric in the seams between units so the pieced border fits evenly along the quilt edge.

For the picket fence border in FENCED IN, I started and finished with a picket, then where necessary, made a slight adjustment to the size by shaving ⅛" off the railing units to ensure a good fit. By doing it this way, the adjustments are hardly noticeable when the border is finished.

All it takes is a little adjustment here and there, and everything works out just fine.

Fabric	Strips	1ˢᵗ cut	2ⁿᵈ cut	No.	Unit assembly

Inner Borders

Muslin		1½"	68½"	2	
Muslin		1½"	46½"	2	

Measure your quilt and make sure the 2nd cut measurement agrees with your own quilt's measurements at this stage.

Sew these strips to the picket fence border before adding the two longer strips to the sides.

Picket Fence Corners

Muslin	2	4"	35"	2	

Sew to both sides of a 1½" x 35" strip of medium dark scraps used for the blocks.

Cut the strips into 4–8½" squares. (These squares are slightly larger than needed, but it is easier to trim back to the required measurement.)

Cut two of the squares at a 45° angle from top left to bottom right then cut the other two squares in the opposite direction – bottom left to top right.

Take this next stage slowly. Sew two opposing angles together. To ensure that the railings match, place your ruler so that it measures 2¼" of fabric below and to the outer side of the railings; trim these two edges.

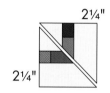

2¼"

2¼"

Turn and trim the other two sides to make a 6½" square. Add this square to each end of the top and bottom fence border.

Outer Border

Once again check your quilt's dimensions by measuring down the center and both sides before cutting and attaching the side borders. Next, measure across the center and both ends before cutting and attaching the top and bottom borders.

Choose a dark fabric that brings out the best color in the quilt.

Dark		2½"	80½"	2	

Attach to each side.

Dark		2½"	62½"	2	

Attach to top and bottom.

Binding

Dark		2½"	305"		

(refer to Binding, pg. 30)

FENCED IN

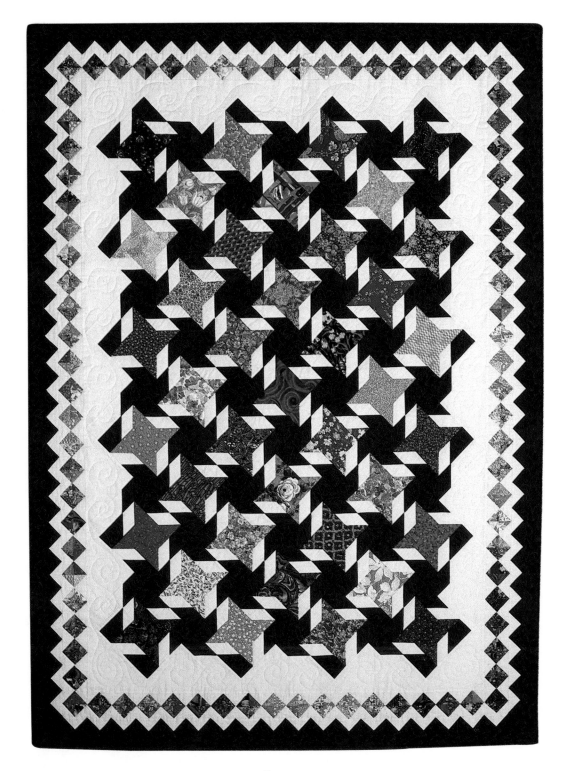

FIFESHIRE
(Pieced by Becky Hamilton; machine quilted by Bev Dyke)

FIFESHIRE uses muslin and a dark blue to coordinate with all the scrap squares in the centers of the stars. Bring your own influence to your quilt by changing values in the blocks or using dark scraps to replace the dark blue. Or, change the background to a splotchy fabric that has movement. The variations are endless! The pieced border is not for beginners!

F
i
f
e
s
h
i
r
e

FIFESHIRE

Finished size: 61" x 84"
Finished block size: 8"
Number of blocks: 39 (4 x 6
                             set on point)

Fabric Required

Muslin . . . . 3 yards
Dark . . . . 2½ yards
Scraps (minimum per block) . 5" x 10"

Basic block

Finished units required for each block

Center square
A (x1)

Half Rec-1R
B (x4)

Unit	Fabric	1ˢᵗ cut	2ⁿᵈ cut	No.	Unit assembly
A	Medium	4½"	4½"	1	

- *Using a 5" x 10" piece of scrap, cut the 4½" square first then the four 2½" squares from the remainder.*

Unit	Fabric	1ˢᵗ cut	2ⁿᵈ cut	No.	Unit assembly
B	Dark	2½"	4½"	4	
	Light	2½"	4½"	4	
	Medium	2½"	2½"	4	

Bonus Tri-2

Bonus Tri-2

The pieced border for FIFESHIRE uses Bonus Tri-2s from Unit B. But, when marking for Bonus Tri-2s, use only ⅜" space (rather than the usual ½") between lines and sew on the seam allowance side of both lines. This will give you Bonus Tri-2s that should measure 2" and need little trimming. Test these bonus triangles after you have sewn a few so you can make the necessary adjustments to yield a 2" unit.

Complete blocks using the Start-a-Seam method, as follows:

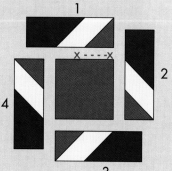

Fabric	1ˢᵗ cut	2ⁿᵈ cut	No.
Side Setting Units			
Muslin	2½"	7½"	16
Dark	2½"	4½"	16

Unit assembly

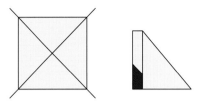

Side Setting Triangles

Muslin	13½"	13½"	4

Cut into fourths diagonally to make 16 triangles.

Add one pieced side setting unit to the left side of each of 16 triangles as shown.

 There will be an overlap when the triangle units are attached to each end of the rows. Trim these back, keeping a straight line with the row to which it is attached.

Corners

Muslin	10"	10"	2

Cut in half diagonally to make four corner triangles.

Quilt Top Assembly

Make each section as labeled. Once the section is complete, add the corners to A, B, C, and D before sewing the sections together.

Sew A to B, and C to D. Sew AB section to E. Finally, sew CD section to E.

When quilt top is assembled, trim back to measure 48½" x 69½" so your pieced border will fit.

Quilt assembly diagram

Pieced Inner Borders

Trim scrap bonus Tri-2s to 2". You should have 156 scrap and 156 dark units. Extras will be needed to complete the borders.

Fabric		1st cut	2nd cut	No.	Unit assembly

Row 1

Sew the 156 bonus scrap Tri-2s into 39 units of four Tri-2s as shown. Make 43 additional units.

C	Various scraps	2⅞"	2⅞"	86	
	Muslin	2⅞"	2⅞"	86	

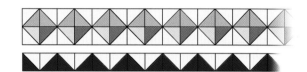

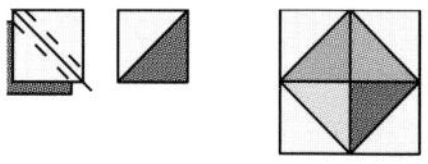

Row 2

Sew the 156 dark Tri-2s into 78 units of two Tri-2s. Make 8 additional units.

D	Muslin	2⅞"	2⅞"	8	
	Dark	2⅞"	2⅞"	8	

Sides

Sew 23 C units together. Sew 23 D units together. Join these two rows before attaching to either side.

Top and Bottom

Sew 18 C units together; add a unit D to each end as shown. Sew 18 D units together; cut four dark 2" squares and attach to both ends. Join the two rows together and attach to the top and bottom.

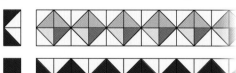

Outer Border

Fabric	1st cut	2nd cut	No.
Dark	2½"	78½"	2

Attach to sides.

Dark	2½"	61½"	2

Attach to top and bottom.

Binding

Scrap	2½"	300"

(refer to Binding, pg. 30)

FLANNEL FLOWERS
(Pieced and hand quilted by Joyce Jones)

When I designed this quilt intending to use flannels, I did it knowing there had already been a lot of negative comments about the difficulties of working with flannels. Most suggestions said not to make any pieces smaller than three inches. But, I had already cut the 1½" units, and found flannel lovely to work with. Yes, it stretches a little if you are not careful, but it is also very forgiving. The result is extremely pleasing – a real "comforter."

FLANNEL FLOWERS

Finished size:	59" x 70"
Finished block size:	9"
Number of blocks:	20 (4 x 5)
First border:	1⅜"
Second border:	5"

Fabric Required

Dark #1	.2 yards
Light #1	1¾ yards
Floral	.2 yards
Dark #2	¼ yard
Light #2	¼ yard
Plaid	¼ yard

Keep the values of Light #1 and #2 as close as possible so a "flower" pattern emerges.

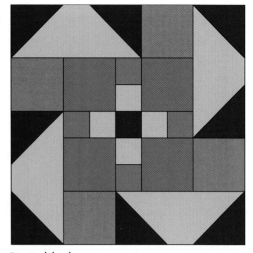

Basic block

Finished units required for each block

   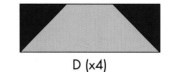

A (x4) B (x1) C (x4) D (x4) E (x4)

Cutting instructions are for the entire quilt.

Unit	Fabric	Strips	1ˢᵗ cut	2ⁿᵈ cut	No.	Unit assembly
Block Center						
A	Light #1	3	1½"		96	
	Medium	3	1½"		96	

• *Sew in strips then cut into 96, 1½" units.*

B	Dark #1	1	1½"	1½"	24	

• *Attach the B square between two A units as shown.*

C	Floral	5	2½"	2½"	96	

• *Assemble block center as shown.*

Save four block centers for use later as border corners.

Unit	Fabric	Strips	1st cut	2nd cut	No.
D	Light #1	12	2½"	5½"	80
	Dark #1	10	2½"	2½"	160

Unit assembly

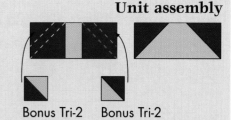

Bonus Tri-2   Bonus Tri-2

 FLANNEL FLOWERS has a pieced border that uses Bonus Tri-2 units leftover from making Unit D. But, in order to ensure that the Bonus Tri-2s are large enough, mark your stitching lines ⅜" apart rather than the usual ½" and sew to the seam allowance side of the line. The resulting Tri-2s should be 1⅞". Check for accuracy after making a few.

Unit	Fabric	Strips	1st cut	2nd cut	No.
E	Light #2	5	2½"	2½"	80

- *Add an E square to the right side of D units as shown.*

Block Construction

Using the Start-a-Seam method, sew together as shown.

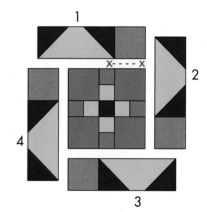

	Fabric	Strips	1st cut	2nd cut	No.
Sashing					
	Dark #1	13	2½"	9½"	49

Sew vertical sashing at the beginning, end, and between blocks as shown.

Assemble five rows of four blocks each.

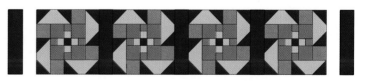

Connector Squares

	Fabric	Strips	1st cut	2nd cut	No.
	Plaid	2	2½"	2½"	30

Sew horizontal sashing strips together with connector squares. Add strips to top, bottom, and between rows as shown.

 Because of the way the triangles fit the corners, the first section of border sashing on each side of the corner is slightly smaller (8¼") than the middle border sashing (8½"). When attaching these borders, the triangle sets will center over the small connector squares in the sashing. Pin these carefully in place then ease when sewing. If you are using flannel fabric, it is very easy to push-me-pull-me.

Pieced Borders

Trim 44 Bonus Tri-2s to 1⅞" and sew into sets of two as shown.

Fabric	Strips	1ˢᵗ cut	2ⁿᵈ cut	No.
Light	4	1⅞"	8¼"	8
Light		1⅞"	8½"	10
Light		1⅞"	1⅞"	4

Side pieces

Make two inner border strips as follows and attach to each side of the quilt top, centering triangles over connector squares.

Top and bottom pieces

Make two inner border strips as follows. Add small squares to each end then attach to the top and bottom of the quilt, centering triangles over connector squares.

Outer Border

Floral	5½"	58¼"	2	Attach to each side.	
Floral	5½"	49¼"	2	Attach the squares saved from making the block centers to each end before adding to the top and bottom of the quilt.	

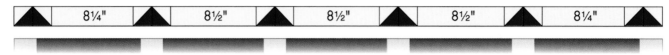

 If the quilt top seems to have slight added fullness, sew with the fullness underneath so the feed dogs help even it out.

Binding

Cut your choice of binding, 2½" x 270" (refer to Binding, pg. 30).

Quilting for FLANNEL FLOWERS

After pin basting, flannel gives you a great excuse to practice a Big Stitch (three or four to the inch). This looked far better than I had hoped and it was extremely quick to do. Using No. 8 Perle cotton and a chenille needle, quilt ¼" inside the outline of the block "flower," but ditch stitch around the four light center squares.

At this stage I felt there still wasn't quite enough quilting so I added a double cross stitch at the junction of the light and floral squares in the center square. This finished the block off nicely. I did the same thing around the four corners of the connector squares. The only other hand quilting on the top was inside the sashing connector squares.

FLANNEL FLOWERS

GENTLE ANNIE
(Pieced by Anne Day; machine quilted by Bev Dyke)

In GENTLE ANNIE, the use of soft pastel scrap blocks set on point gives it an antique look. Vary the greens and apricots as much as possible using calico-type prints. Making the blocks generated enough Bonus Tri-2s to complete the pieced outer border with two extra! GENTLE ANNIE has a Design Double Take in RICHMOND ROUNDABOUT (pg. 73).

Uncovering Traditional Quilts – Joyce Jones

GENTLE ANNIE

Finished size: 84" x 99"
Finished block size: 12"
Number of blocks: 32
                        (set on point)

Fabric Required

Muslin . . . . .7 yards
Multi-scraps for Unit A, inner 1"
borders and binding
    Greens . . . . 10" square
    Apricots . . . . 10" square

Basic block

Finished units required for each block

A (x1)   B (x4)   C (x4)   D (x4)

Unit	Fabric	1st cut	2nd cut	No.	Unit assembly
A	Scrap	1½"	Strips	16 (x32)	

• *Make at least six different sets of strips to add placement variety.*

Unit	Fabric	1st cut	2nd cut	No.	Unit assembly
B	Green	4⅞"	4⅞"	2	
	Apricot	4⅞"	4⅞"	2	
	Muslin	2½"	2½"	8	

• *Make Tri-2s then Squiffy muslin squares to the corners.*

Bonus Tri-2   Bonus Tri-2

Unit	Fabric	1st cut	2nd cut	No.	Unit assembly
C	Muslin	2½"	4½"	4	
	Green	2½"	2½"	8	

(See instructions for making Flying Geese units, pg. 19)

Bonus Tri-2

The pieced border for GENTLE ANNIE uses Bonus Tri-2s left over from making Units B and C. To make certain the bonus Tri-2s are the required 1⅞", mark the sewing lines ⅜" apart rather than the usual ½"; sew on the seam allowance side of both lines.

Unit	Fabric	1st cut	2nd cut	No.	Unit assembly
D	Apricot	2½"	4½"	4	

• *Attach to C units as shown.*

Gentle Annie

GENTLE ANNIE

Block Assembly

Sew units together as shown in rows of three, then sew rows together to form the block.

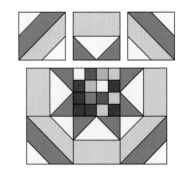

Side Setting Triangles

The triangles are cut larger than necessary making the blocks appear to "float." Note also that each side setting triangle has two Squiffies attached at the tip to form a square at the junction of the blocks.

When attaching side setting triangles, the lower edges of the triangles should meet with no "overhang." To ensure this, start sewing the seam, then go to the bottom of the two triangles and pin or hold so the bias edge remains stable.

Fabric	1st cut	2nd cut	No.
Muslin	18"	18"	4

(This produces 16 triangles, but only 14 are required.)

Make sure the first cut is on the straight grain of the fabric to avoid distortion when triangles are attached. Spray starching the bias seams before stitching helps prevent distortion. Carefully cut each square diagonally into four triangles.

Green	4½"	4½"	14

Squiffy the green square to the muslin triangle. Flip, check, and trim.

Muslin	2½"	2½"	14

Squiffy the muslin square to the green triangle. Flip and check before trimming.

Corners

Muslin	10½"	10½"	2

Cut in half diagonally.

Unit assembly

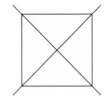

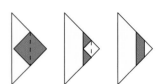

Quilt Top Assembly

Arrange blocks on point. Sew the top by constructing diagonal rows first, then attaching the side setting triangles for those particular rows.

Join the rows together, adding the corner sections last. Fold corner triangle in half and match the fold line over the center of the corner block.

Check that the quilt top is laying flat and that the edges of the side setting triangles are even before squaring off the corners.

Measure your quilt top down the center and both sides to find the length. Measure across the middle as well as the top and bottom, to find the width. If necessary, trim to 69" x 85".

Quilt assembly diagram

Scrap Inner Border

Sew 1" strips of multi-colored scraps together to make inner borders.

Fabric	1st cut	2nd cut	No.	
Scraps	1"	85"	2	Sew one strip to each side of the quilt.
Scraps	1"	70"	2	Sew strips to the top and bottom.

Pin strips securely at the start and end of rows to ensure a good fit.

Pieced Border

If you haven't already done so, trim all Bonus Tri-2s to 1⅞". After measuring your quilt top, you may discover a pieced border won't fit exactly. To reduce a pieced border slightly to make it fit, "pinch" a little extra off the seams between pieced units. So that it will show less, take the extra off many seams rather than a few.

Row 1

Sew the first row as shown. Each side uses 62 Tri-2 units. The top and bottom edges each use 50 Tri-2 units. You may find it easier to sew units in sets of two before sewing them all together.

Row 2

Unit	Fabric	1st cut	2nd cut	No.
Spacers	Muslin	1⅞"	3¼"	54

Sew second border row as shown. Each side uses 32 Tri-2 units plus 15 muslin spacers. Top and bottom rows use 26 Tri-2 units plus 12 muslin spacers. Start and finish with Tri-2 units.

Sew the first and second pieced rows together to form two sides (see outer edge border diagram). Attach to each side of the quilt top.

Corner Squares

Cut four 3¼" muslin squares for the corners. Squiffy a 1⅞" scrap square to one corner of each muslin square to make a Sq-1.

Add a corner square to the ends of both top and bottom sections before attaching to the quilt top.

Outer Border

	Muslin	5½"	92½"	2	Attach to sides.
	Muslin	5½"	86½"	2	Attach to top and bottom.

Binding

	Scrap	2½"	386"		(refer to Binding, pg. 30)

Design Double Take

Gentle Annie

Basic block

RICHMOND ROUNDABOUT

(Pieced by Joyce Jones;
machine quilted by Bev Dyke)
Finished size: 53" x 65"
Finished block size: 12"
Number of blocks: 12 (3 x 4)

RICHMOND ROUNDABOUT uses the same block design as GENTLE ANNIE, but the look is much different. Strong use of green and red, plus a little yellow and black, gives this quilt vibrancy. It definitely needed the scrap strip inner border. In GENTLE ANNIE, the blocks are set on point and use muslin and scrap for a total contrast.

K
i
w
i

F
e
a
t
h
e
r
s

KIWI FEATHERS
(Pieced by Becky Hamilton; machine quilted by Bev Dyke)

So many different things could be done with this quilt. Start at one point of KIWI FEATHERS shown above and follow the line through until you reach the start again. Imagine how you could use your color preferences. Color could also be run through the "Figure-8s" in the blocks. PIGEON VALLEY (pg. 77) uses the same block design but has an intriguing "barber pole" inner border with an outside border of blocks.

KIWI FEATHERS

Finished size: 49" x 67"
Finished block size: 8"
Number of blocks: 24 (4 x 6)

Fabric Required

Batik print (inner border) . . . ¼ yard
Main dark . . . . 2¼ yards
(for sashings, borders, and binding)
Scrap (minimum per block)
 Lights . . . . 3" x 22"
 Mediums . . . . 1½" x 21"
 Darks . . . . 1½" x 24"

Basic block

Finished units required for each block

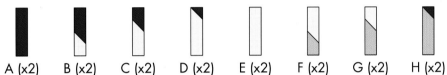

A (x2) B (x2) C (x2) D (x2) E (x2) F (x2) G (x2) H (x2)

Cutting instructions are for one block. Use as many different fabrics as possible for A – H.

Unit	Fabric	1st cut	2nd cut	No.	Unit assembly
A	Dark	1½"	4½"	2	
B	Dark	1½"	3½"	2	
	Light	1½"	2½"	2	
C	Dark	1½"	2½"	2	
	Light	1½"	3½"	2	
D	Dark	1½"	1½"	2	
	Light	1½"	4½"	2	

- *When using Squiffies, whenever possible draw your stitching line on the lighter fabrics. For darker fabrics, soap slivers work well.*

Unit	Fabric	1st cut	2nd cut	No.	Unit assembly
E	Light	1½"	4½"	2	
F	Light	1½"	3½"	2	
	Medium	1½"	2½"	2	
G	Light	1½"	2½"	2	
	Medium	1½"	3½"	2	
H	Medium	1½"	4½"	2	
	Dark	1½"	1½"	2	

Block Construction

Assemble A-D units and E-H units as shown. Pair units and then sew pairs together.

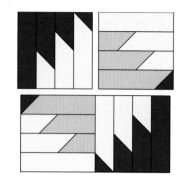

When making scrap blocks, it helps to do quite a number and lay them out to see how the colors blend together. This is a good time to assess whether there is enough of, for example, blue or red, and answer the question: Would a few blocks of yellow brighten the whole effect?

Fabric	1st cut	2nd cut	No.

Sashing
| Main dark | 1½" | 8½" | 38 |

Add a sashing strip vertically between blocks. Dark sashing will probably work best. The small connecting squares (1½") can be scrap or coordinated fabric.

Connector Squares
| Mixed | 1½" | 1½" | 15 |

Add connector squares between horizontal sashing pieces as shown, and attach the sashing strips between rows of blocks.

First Border
| Main dark | 2¾" | 53½" | 2 |
| Main dark | 2¾" | 40" | 2 |

Attach long pieces to sides and short pieces to top and bottom.

Second Border
| Batik print | 1¼" | 58" | 2 |
| Batik print | 1¼" | 41½" | 2 |

Sew to sides, then top and bottom.

Outer Border
| Main dark | 4½" | 59½" | 2 |
| Main dark | 4½" | 49½" | 2 |

Sew to sides, then top and bottom.

Binding
| Main dark | 2½" | 242" | |

(see Binding, pg. 30)

KIWI FEATHERS

Design Double Take

PIGEON VALLEY

(Pieced and machine quilted by Nan Batty)

Finished size: 86" x 102"
Finished block size: 8"
Number of blocks: 88

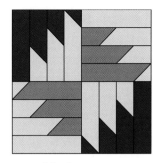

Basic block

It is the border that makes this quilt vastly different from
KIWI FEATHERS. Nan had decided to do a wallhanging using this design until she saw
the border I designed. Inspired, she doubled PIGEON VALLEY's size by adding another
40 blocks to form the border and added a "barber pole" inner border – more than double the trouble, but the result was worth it! The unusual border gives this quilt "show
stopper" appeal. Instructions for making the "barber pole" border are on pg. 78.

Barber Pole Border for PIGEON VALLEY

PIGEON VALLEY'S unusual inner and outer borders make this a fascinating quilt. The "barber pole" border is bias cut from narrow strips of fabric. You will need six fabrics for this border. Cut one 1" strip the full width of each fabric (42"), plus another 25" strip of the same fabrics. PIGEON VALLEY used the following: dark, medium, light, and a second dark, medium, and light.

Barber Pole Border

Fabric	1ˢᵗ cut	2ⁿᵈ cut	No.
Six fabrics	1"	42"	1 each
Six fabrics	1"	25"	1 each

Sew the pieces of each fabric together to make a strip 65" long. Then attach the strips together to make a 65" piece, 3½" wide. Fuse to a fine, lightweight iron-on facing to stabilize the fabric, then cut at a 45-degree angle into 1" strips.

If you would like to use more than six strips, measure the depth of the row you have sewn. Disregard the half-inch seam allowance and multiply by 1.414. This will be the finished length yielded in the bias cutting. Divide the total needed by this amount to find how many segments are required.

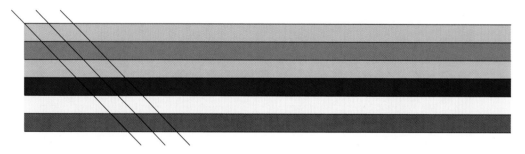

3" x 1.414 = 4¼" length of finished yield (this allows for seams).

One 42" strip will yield 4¼" x 37" = 157" of bias barber pole stripe.

Sew bias cut strips together to make border pieces.

KOWHAI
(Pieced by Joyce Jones; machine quilted by Bev Dyke)

This block has a great many possibilities. In this case, four blocks are joined to form a "flower." The design is reminiscent of the New Zealand Kowhai flower which attracts the honey-seeking, white-throated Tui. Before sewing the quilt top together, play with the blocks to form many other patterns. Make it in scrap, with sashing between, or set the colors in columns. Once you start, the settings will surprise you.

KOWHAI

Finished size: 85" x 105"
Finished block size: 10"
Number of blocks: 48 (6 x 8)

Fabric Required

Blue. . . . . 1¾ yards
Cream . . . . 1¾ yards
Gold . . . . 1¾ yards
Brown . . . . 3½ yards
Dark blue . . . . 3 yards
Binding . . . . 1¾ yards

Basic block

Finished units required for each block

Center   Sq-2   Rec-1R
A (x1)   B (x4)   C (x4)

Cutting directions are for all 48 blocks.

Unit	Fabric	Strips	1ˢᵗ cut	2ⁿᵈ cut	No.	Unit assembly
A	Dark blue	3	2½"	2½"	48	
B	Cream	6	4½"	4½"	48	
	Gold	3	2½"	2½"	48	
	Dark blue	3	2½"	2½"	48	Bonus Tri-2s
	Gold	6	4½"	4½"	48	
	Brown	3	2½"	2½"	48	
	Dark blue	3	2½"	2½"	48	Bonus Tri-2s
	Brown	6	4½"	4½"	48	
	Blue	3	2½"	2½"	48	
	Dark blue	3	2½"	2½"	48	Bonus Tri-2s
	Blue	6	4½"	4½"	48	
	Cream	3	2½"	2½"	48	
	Dark blue	3	2½"	2½"	48	Bonus Tri-2s

Bonus Tri-2 units – As with any of the patterns in this book, you always have the choice to make or not make bonus Tri-2s. In KOWHAI, *each block yields 12 bonus Tri-2s, giving you 576. I used*

two rows of bonus Tri-2s in the diamond border. Yes, it was fiddly, but well worth it. I would never have considered making that many after having done the quilt top, so to have them pre-made was a definite "bonus." To avoid having too many to do at once, trim the bonus Tri-2s as you go.

When marking each Squiffy for sewing, make a second mark ⅜" from the first rather than the usual ½". Sew on the seam allowance side of both lines. This will ensure that the resulting bonus Tri-2 will be the required 1⅞". Check your work for accuracy after making a few units.

Unit	Fabric	Strips	1ˢᵗ cut	2ⁿᵈ cut	No.	Unit assembly
C	Cream	6	2½"	4½"	48	Bonus Tri-2
	Dark blue	3	2½"	2½"	48	
	Gold	6	2½"	4½"	48	Bonus Tri-2
	Dark blue	3	2½"	2½"	48	
	Brown	6	2½"	4½"	48	Bonus Tri-2
	Dark blue	3	2½"	2½"	48	
	Blue	6	2½"	4½"	48	Bonus Tri-2
	Dark blue	3	2½"	2½"	48	

Block Construction

Take note of the color placement in the block and join corresponding B and C units. For example:

The gold Rec-1R to the left of the brown Sq-2.
The brown Rec-1R to the left of the blue Sq-2.

The blue Rec-1R to the left of the cream Sq-2.
The cream Rec-1R to the left of the gold Sq-2.

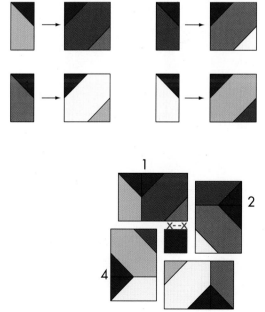

Using the Start-a-Seam method, assemble the blocks. See instructions for Start-a-Seam on pg. 23.

Pieced Inner Border

Trim Bonus Tri-2s to $1\frac{7}{8}$" and sew 408 Tri-2s into pairs to form diamonds as shown.

Sew together 58 of the diamond units and attach to each side of the quilt.

Fabric	1ˢᵗ cut	2ⁿᵈ cut	No.	Assembly
Pieced Inner Border Corners				
Brown	$3\frac{1}{4}$"	$3\frac{1}{4}$"	4	Sew together two rows of 44 diamond units and attach a brown square to each end before stitching the pieced border to the top and bottom of the quilt.
Border 2				
Dark blue	$2\frac{1}{4}$"	86"	2	Sew strips to both sides of the quilt top.
Brown	$2\frac{1}{4}$"	$2\frac{1}{4}$"	4	Add a brown corner to each end of the blue strips and sew to the top and bottom of the quilt.
Dark blue	$2\frac{1}{4}$"	66"	2	
Outer Border				
Brown	$8\frac{1}{2}$"	$89\frac{1}{2}$"	2	Attach to each side of the quilt top.
Brown	$8\frac{1}{2}$"	$69\frac{1}{2}$"	2	Add a corner (shown below) to each end before attaching to the top and bottom of the quilt.

Corner Pinwheel Blocks

Fabric	1ˢᵗ cut	2ⁿᵈ cut	No.
Brown	$2\frac{1}{2}$"	$4\frac{1}{2}$"	4
Brown	$2\frac{1}{2}$"	$2\frac{1}{2}$"	8
Blue	$2\frac{1}{2}$"	$4\frac{1}{2}$"	4

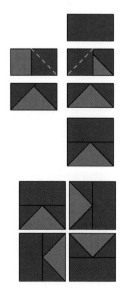

To form corner blocks, sew rectangles to Flying Geese units then make the four into a block.

Binding

Dark blue $2\frac{1}{2}$"   390"
(refer to Binding, pg. 30)

Design Double Takes

COVER STORY

(Pieced by Joyce Jones)

APPLEBY BLUES

(Pieced by Rhoda Cohen)

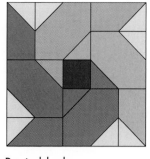

Basic block
COVER STORY

Basic block
APPLEBY BLUES

Finished size:	30" x 45" without borders
Finished block size:	7½"
Number of blocks:	24 (4 x 6)

One Block – Three Quilts. KOWHAI, COVER STORY, and APPLEBY BLUES all use the same block design but with dramatically different results. KOWHAI has its own drama, using colors that vary from blues through yellows, and keeping to a flower form contained within four blocks. For APPLEBY BLUES, Rhoda Cohen used her amazing collection of fabrics to make the pattern drift in and out of perspective. APPLEBY BLUES is not a quilt to be "read" in one sitting. COVER STORY, on the other hand, stayed within the black and white range with hints of blue-beige. Both of these quilts have arms of color stretching into the next area to create an Escher-like movement that takes your eye onto each new step. Auditioning as you go is a must with both quilts.

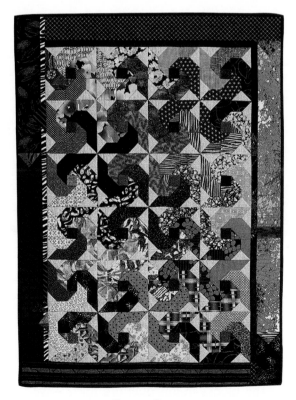

COVER STORY

APPLEBY BLUES

M
a
r
b
l
e

M
o
u
n
t
a
i
n

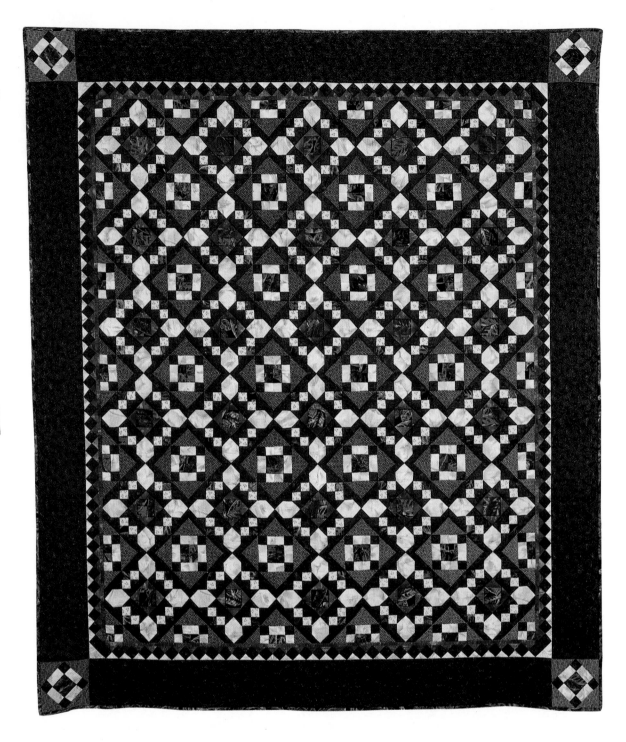

MARBLE MOUNTAIN
(Pieced, machine and hand quilted by Carolyn McKay)

This lovely block is fun to make. The main unit is constructed in a unique way to avoid unnecessary seam lines. The larger marble rectangle has a Goose's End unit at one end and a Tri-4 effect at the other. Another great advantage is that almost all of the pieced border units are made from bonus Tri-4 units constructed at the same time as the block. The blocks in this quilt are fairly easy, but the borders do need a little manipulation.

Uncovering Traditional Quilts – Joyce Jones

MARBLE MOUNTAIN

Finished size: 80" x 93"
Finished block size: 12½"
Number of blocks: 30 (5 x 6)

Fabric Required

Marble . . . . 2½ yards
Light print . . . . ¾ yard
Dark #1 . . . . 5½ yards
Focal print . . . . 1¾ yards
Check . . . . 1 yard
Dark #2 . . . . 1 yard

Basic block

Finished units required for each block

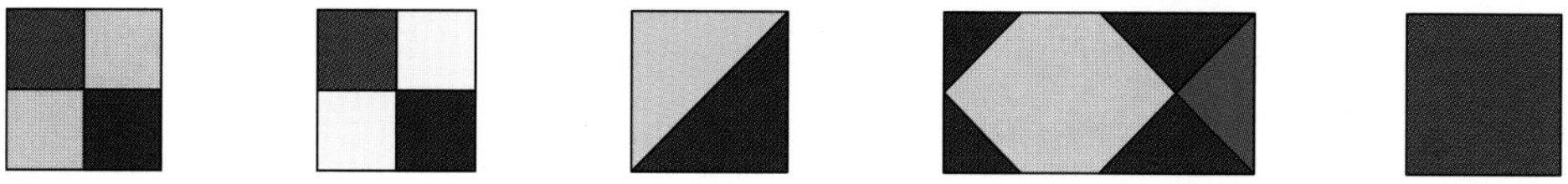

4-Patch   4-Patch   Tri-2   Goose's End/Tri-4   Center
A (x4)   B (x4)   C (x4)   D (x4)   E (x1)

The following cutting instructions are for the full quilt.

Unit	Fabric	Strips	1st cut	2nd cut	No.	Unit assembly
A	Focal print	6	1¾"	1¾"	120	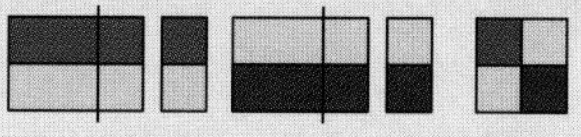
	Marble	12	1¾"	1¾"	240	
	Dark #1	6	1¾"	1¾"	120	
B	Focal print	6	1¾"	1¾"	120	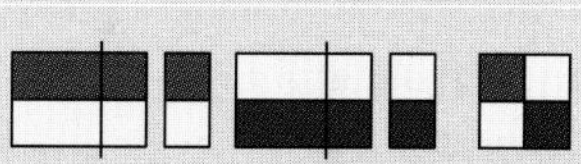
	Light print	12	1¾"	1¾"	240	
	Dark #1	6	1¾"	1¾"	120	
C	Check	6	3⅜"	3⅜"	60	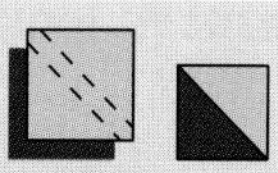
	Dark #1	6	3⅜"	3⅜"	60	
D	Marble	18	3"	5½"	120	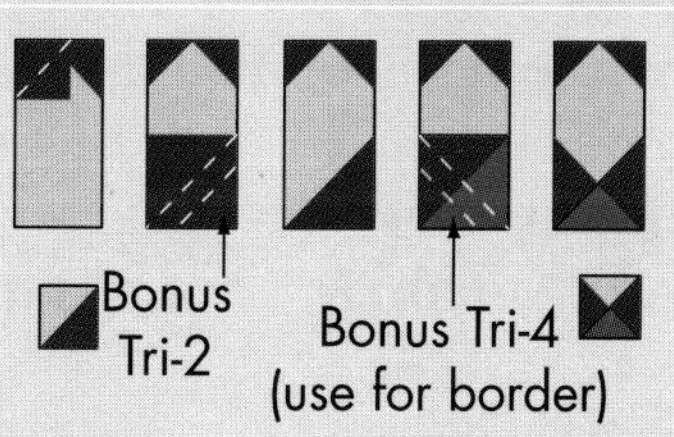
	Dark #1	12	1¾"	1¾"	240	

• *Make Goose's End points as shown on page 19.*

Unit	Fabric	Strips	1st cut	2nd cut	No.
	Dark #1	13	3"	3"	120
	Dark #1	10	3⅜"	3⅜"	60
	Dark #2	10	3⅜"	3⅜"	60

Bonus Tri-2

Bonus Tri-4
(use for border)

• *Using 3⅜" Dark #1 and Dark #2 squares, make Tri-2 units following the instructions for C, above. Attach to unit D, as shown.*

Unit	Fabric	Strips	1st cut	2nd cut	No.
E	Focal print	3	3"	3"	30 

Block Construction

Sew units together as shown to form each block.

Assemble blocks in rows five blocks wide and six blocks deep.

Pieced Inner Border

Trim Bonus Tri4-s to 2⅜". You will need 142 (40 for each side and 32 for the top and bottom). You should have 120 of these Tri-4 units left over from constructing the blocks. Make another 24 Tri-4s as follows:

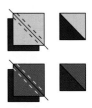

Unit	Fabric	1ˢᵗ cut	2ⁿᵈ cut	No.
Tri-2 A	Marble Dark #1	3¼" 3¼"	3¼" 3¼"	6 6
Tri-2 B	Dark #1 Dark #2	3¼" 3¼"	3¼" 3¼"	6 6

Tri-4   Use one of each A and B Tri-2s. Place them with right sides together, dark to light, and draw your lines ¼" from the center as shown. Sew, check, and cut (see instructions on making Squirty Tri-4s, pg. 11).

 From past experience you may already know that it is nearly impossible to have pieced borders work out to the exact size of the quilt top. Your finished quilt top should measure 63" x 75½". Please check your quilt top by measuring down the middle and both sides (see pg. 31 for instructions on measuring quilt tops for borders). It helps to draw a rectangle and write those measurements on the drawing. Now measure across the middle and across the top and bottom.

MARBLE MOUNTAIN was made to fit the pieced border, as the pieced border is slightly smaller than the quilt top and bottom. If your quilt is larger than 62", take "fractions" off as many seams as you can until the measurement is as close as possible. The rest will be overcome by a little push-me-pull-me! Whenever doing this, make sure you pin securely at the start and finish, places you definitely will want to look perfect.

Trim Tri-4s to 2⅜" to match the bonus Tri-4s. Sew together two lengths of 40 Tri-4s and two lengths of 32 Tri-4s.

Inner Border

Fabric	Strips	1ˢᵗ cut	2ⁿᵈ cut	No.
Tan	2	1"	75½"	2
Tan	2	1"	62"	2

Attach the 75½" tan strips to the tan side of the 40 Tri-4s, pinning at the start, finish and center. Sew these strips, with the tan side to the seam, to each side of the quilt.

Attach the 62" strips to the tan side of each row of 32 Tri-4s. You will have to compromise again here by taking in or letting out fractions on the Tri-4s. Just keep telling yourself it's worth it!

Tri-2 Corners

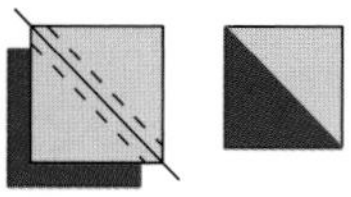

Cut two dark and two marble 3¼" squares. Assemble as shown. Add to the ends of the 62" border units as shown. Attach borders to the top and bottom.

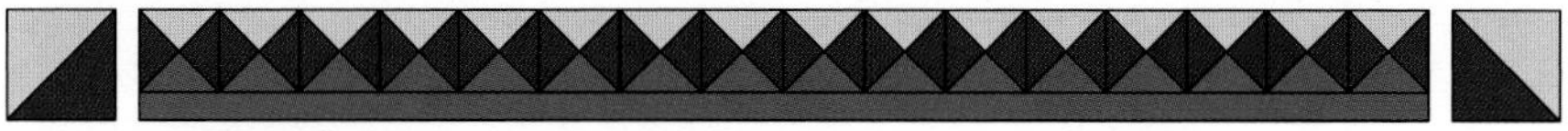

Outer Border Corner Units

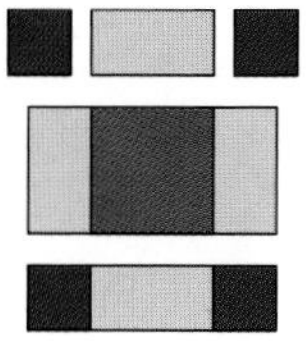

Fabric	1st cut	2nd cut	No.
Focal print	2⅞"	2⅞"	4
Marble	2⅞"	1¾"	16
Dark #1	1¾"	1¾"	16
Check	4⅝"	4⅝"	8

Sew a marble rectangle to each side of the focal print squares. Add a dark square to each end of the remaining rectangles and attach to the top and bottom as illustrated.

Cut check squares into triangles and attach them to the corner units as shown. Fold both the square and the triangle in half to find the center and pin the pieces together before sewing. Attach opposite sides first, then remaining corners.

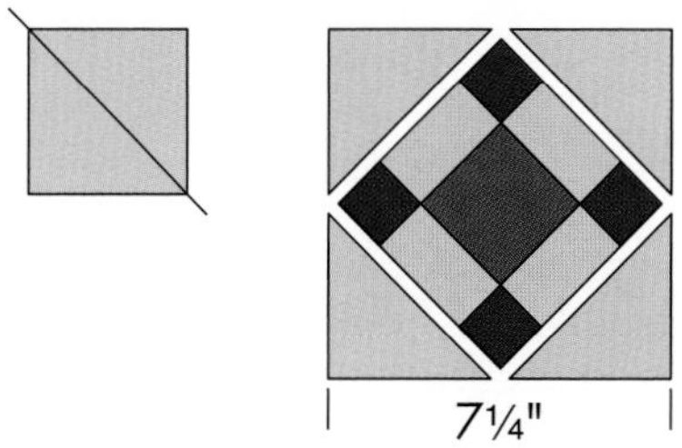

Border

Fabric	1st cut	2nd cut	No.
Dark #1	7¼"	80¼"	2

Add to each side.

Dark #1	7¼"	66¾"	2

Attach corner squares to each end of both strips; attach to the top and bottom of the quilt.

Binding

Focal print	2½"	356"

(see Binding, pg. 30)

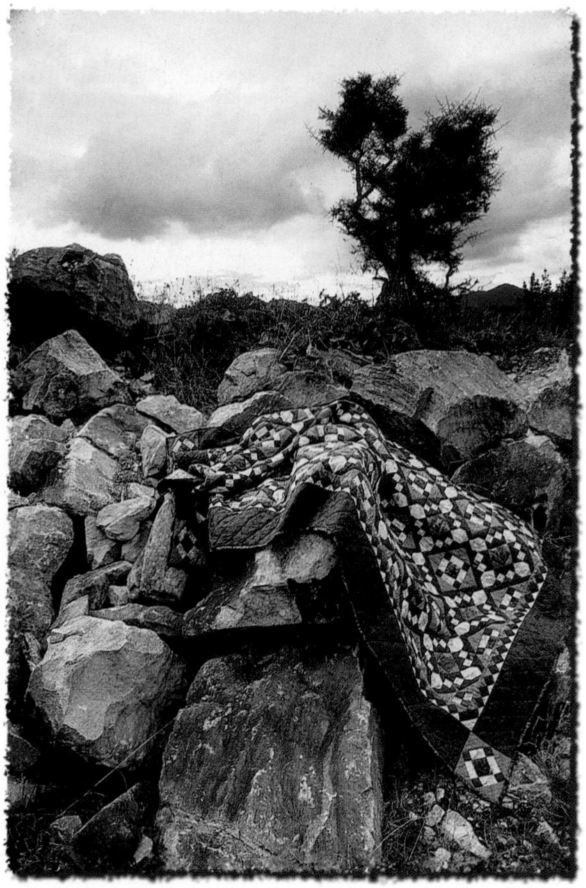

MARBLE MOUNTAIN

M a r s   L a n d i n g

MARS LANDING
(Pieced by Pat Buchanan; machine quilted by Bev Dyke)

To give the impression of stars floating on a background, use the same dark fabric for the side setting triangles as that used in the corners of the blocks. The triangles are slightly larger than necessary to enhance the "floating" effect. The dark background of MARS LANDING makes it difficult to identify how the blocks are oriented; these are set on point.

Uncovering Traditional Quilts – Joyce Jones

Mars Landing

Finished size: 36" x 44"
Finished block size: 6"
Number of blocks: 18
(set on point)

Fabric Required

Dark . . . . 2 yards
Light . . . . ½ yard
Scraps (minimum per block)
    Medium . . . . 4" x 8"

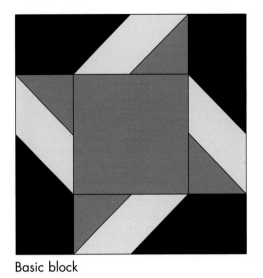

Basic block

Finished units required for each block

Half Rec-1   Center
A (x4)   B (x1)

Cutting instructions for dark and light are for the entire quilt.

Unit	Fabric	Strips	1ˢᵗ cut	2ⁿᵈ cut	No.	Unit assembly
A	Dark	4	2"	2"	72	
	Light	7	2"	3½"	72	
	Medium		2"	2"	4 per block	
B	Medium		3½"	3½"	1 per block	

• *Add 2" Squiffy squares as shown.*

Using the Start-a-Seam method, assemble blocks as shown.

Add each round as illustrated. Finish the original seam, starting at the outer edge and sewing to join with the first seam line.

Uncovering Traditional Quilts – Joyce Jones   89

Setting and Corner Triangles

Fabric	Strips	1ˢᵗ cut	2ⁿᵈ cut	No.
Dark	2	6¾"	45°	10 (plus four corner triangles)

These two strips will yield 10 setting triangles. The corner sections shown in the illustration can be used to make the four corners of the quilt. Just trim them to fit.

Quilt Assembly

Arrange the quilt blocks on point as shown in the Quilt assembly diagram. Add side setting triangles and sew in rows as shown. Each row, when sewn together, will have an overlap of the setting triangles. After making sure the outside edges are even when sewn, the overlap can be trimmed off. Add corner units last.

Corner Blocks for Borders

Cutting instructions are for four blocks. Follow the same assembly instructions as for the main blocks. Corner blocks are the same design, but smaller.

Quilt assembly diagram

Fabric	Strips	1ˢᵗ cut	2ⁿᵈ cut	No.
Dark	1	2½"	2½"	4
Dark	2	1½"	2½"	16
Scrap	2	1½"	2½"	16
Dark	1	1½"	1½"	16

Side Corner Pieced Units

Use various scrap pieces in these units.

Fabric	Strips	1st cut	2nd cut	No.
Scraps		1½"	2½"	12
Dark	1	1½"	1½"	24
Dark		2½"	2½"	4
Dark	1	2½"	5½"	4

Unit assembly

Make four of these sections and place on each side of two diagonally opposite corners as shown in the Quilt assembly diagram. Any necessary adjustments in size can be made to the outer border.

Outer Border

Fabric	Strips	1st cut	2nd cut	No.
Dark	2	4½"	31½"	2
	2	4½"	23"	2

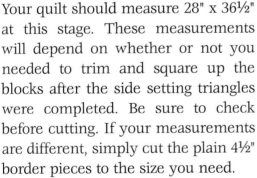

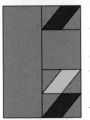

Your quilt should measure 28" x 36½" at this stage. These measurements will depend on whether or not you needed to trim and square up the blocks after the side setting triangles were completed. Be sure to check before cutting. If your measurements are different, simply cut the plain 4½" border pieces to the size you need.

Sew the outer border pieces to the pieced sections and attach to the sides of the quilt. Add corners to either end of the top and bottom border sections before attaching them to the quilt.

Binding

Fabric	1st cut	2nd cut
Dark	2½"	165"

(refer to Binding, pg. 30)

MARS LANDING

O
a
k
l
a
n
d
s

OAKLANDS
(Pieced by Jill Raine; machine quilted by Bev Dyke)

In OAKLANDS, there are 81 pieces in each block, but they are simple to construct. In this case, the Squiffy squares are too small to consider saving as Bonus Tri-2s unless, of course, you enjoy making miniatures, in which case they would be ideal. Note that the border was made to reflect the piecing in the center of the quilt blocks. Even the quilting on the outer edge reflects the nine patches. The rest of the quilting is based on oak leaves and acorns. This quilt was named after Jill's 1842 house, farm property, and many acres of beautiful gardens.

OAKLANDS

Finished size: 73" x 97"
Finished block size: 11"
Number of blocks: 24 (4 x 6)

Fabric Required

Muslin . . . . 7½ yards
Scraps (minimum per block)
    Light . . . . . approx. 12" square
    Floral . . . . . approx. 12" square
    Dark . . . . . approx. 12" square

Basic block

Finished units required for each block

A (x1)   B (x4)   C (x4)

The following cutting instructions are for one block. You may want to bulk cut the muslin for use in all blocks. If so, label the muslin pieces for use with other blocks.

Unit	Fabric	1ˢᵗ cut	2ⁿᵈ cut	No.	Unit assembly
A	Muslin	1½"	1½"	4	
	Light	1½"	1½"	4	
	Dark	1½"	1½"	1	

- *Assemble Unit A by sewing three rows of three pieces together, then connecting the rows as shown.*

B	Muslin	1⅞"	1⅞"	8	
	Floral	1⅞"	1⅞"	8	

- *Make Tri-2s as shown.*

	Floral	2½"	2½"	4	
	Light	1½"	1½"	8	
	Muslin	1½"	1½"	8	

- *Sew strips together, cut into 1½" segments; assemble as shown.*

	Muslin	1½"	2½"	8	

- *To construct the B corner units, sew 1½" x 2½" muslin strips to Tri-2s as shown, being careful in their placement.*

- *Assemble B units as shown.*

Unit	Fabric	1st cut	2nd cut	No.	Unit assembly
C	Dark	1½"	4½"	4	
	Muslin	1½"	1½"	4	
	Light	1½"	4½"	4	
	Dark	1½"	4½"	4	
	Muslin	1½"	1½"	4	

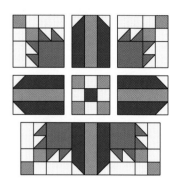

- *Construct C units as shown.*

Block Construction

Sew A, B, and C units together as shown at right.

Sashing

Cutting instructions are for the entire quilt.

Fabric	1st cut	2nd cut	No.
Muslin	1½"	11½"	38
Scraps	1½"	1½"	15

Sew muslin sashing strips between blocks as shown.

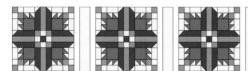

Construct horizontal sashing rows as shown below.

Inner Pieced Borders

Unit	Fabric	1st cut	2nd cut	No.
X, Y, Z	Scraps	1½"	1½"	404
	Muslin	1½"	1½"	336

Using 1½" scrap and muslin squares, assemble:

 68 X units

 20 Y units

 4 Z units

OAKLANDS

Muslin for Pieced Borders

Unit	Fabric	1st cut	2nd cut	No.
D	Muslin	2½"	9½"	28
E	Muslin	1½"	3½"	4
F	Muslin	3½"	3½"	44
G	Muslin	3½"	4½"	4
H	Muslin	3½"	9½"	40
I	Muslin	2½"	6½"	4

Once you have made the X, Y, and Z units and cut the muslin, it is easier to sew the three pieced border rows together before attaching to both sides and finally to the top and bottom.

Side Pieced Borders

Row 1 (make 2) – Z, then six D units separated by five Y units. Finish with a Z unit.

Row 2 (make 2) – E, then 12 X units, separated by 11 F units. Finish with an E unit.

Row 3 (make 2) – G, then six X units, separated by five H units. Finish with a G unit.

Sew rows 1, 2, and 3 together. Attach to either side of the quilt top.

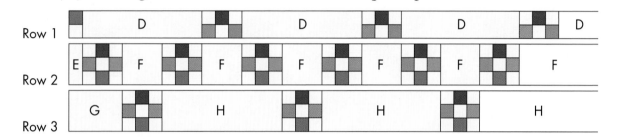

Top and Bottom Pieced Border

Row 1 (make 2) – I, then five Y units separated with four D units. Finish with an I unit.

Row 2 (make 2) – F, then 10 X units, separated with nine F units. Finish with an F unit.

Row 3 (make 2) – X, then five H units separated with four X units. Finish with an X unit.

Sew rows 1, 2, and 3 together. Attach to the top and bottom of the quilt top.

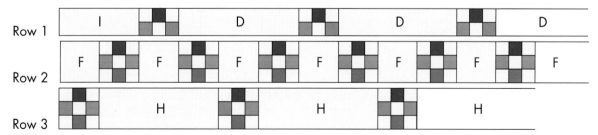

Outer Border

Muslin	5½"	87½"	2	Attach to either side
Muslin	5½"	73½"	2	Attach to the top and bottom.

Binding

Mixed scraps	2½"	350"	(refer to Binding, pg. 30)

PERPETUAL MOTION
(Pieced and machine quilted by Carol Greig)

There are so many possibilities with this quilt. Change the colors for real drama. Black and white would look great or you could use primary colors with a "kiddie" print as the focal. It would be ideal in Christmas colors. Using a border print fabric in the blocks of PERPETUAL MOTION led to using the same fabric in borders for the quilt. This is not a quilt for a beginner! Special care is required to match star points.

Perpetual Motion

Finished size: 48" x 56"
Finished block size: 4"
Number of blocks: 63 (7 x 9)

Fabric Required

Dark . . . . 1 yard
Light . . . . 1 yard
Medium strip . . . . 2½" x 35"
  (for 14 outer Block Cs)
Medium scraps . . . . 12–8" squares
Focal print scraps 12–4½" squares
Border print. . . . . 1¾ yards

Block arrangement

Finished blocks required for quilt

A (x20)   B (x12)   C (x31)

The following cutting instructions are for the entire quilt.

Block	Fabric	Strips	1st cut	2nd cut	No.	Unit assembly
A	Light	2	1½"		40	
	Dark	2	1½"		40	

• *Sew into strips then cut into 1½" segments and assemble as shown into 20 Four-patch units.*

| | Light | | 1½" | 3½" | 40 | |
| | Dark | | 1½" | 1½" | 40 | |

• *Make into Rec-1Ls as shown.*

| | Light | | 1½" | 3½" | 40 | |
| | Dark | | 1½" | 3½" | 40 | |

• *Using the Start-a-Seam method, assemble Block A as shown.*

Block	Fabric	Strips	1ˢᵗ cut	2ⁿᵈ cut	No.	Unit assembly
B	12 Focal print		4½"	4½"	1	
	12 Mediums		2½"	2½"	4	

- *(See pg. 15 for Square-in-a-Square assembly.)*

C	Light	2	4⅞"	4⅞"	16	
	Dark	2	4⅞"	4⅞"	16	

- *Lay out blocks A, B and the Tri-2 stage of Block C as shown below, then follow the instructions for adding Squiffies onto Block Cs before sewing the blocks together.*

Block arrangement diagram

	Medium scraps		2½"	2½"	4 (x 12)	

- *Sew Squiffies to Block Cs to form star points around each Block B.*

	Medium strip		2½"	2½"	14	

- *Attach these Squiffies to the remaining C blocks to form the outer edge.*

PERPETUAL MOTION

Borders

Fabric	1ˢᵗ cut	2ⁿᵈ cut	No.
Dark	2"	36½"	2

Attach to either side of the quilt top.

Dark	2"	31½"	2

Attach to the top and bottom of the quilt.

Border print	7½"	53½"	2

Attach to either side of the quilt.

Border print	7½"	45½"	2

Attach to the top and bottom.

Cut all borders the full length of the finished quilt and miter the corners (see section on Mitering, pg. 28).

Binding

Dark	2½"	205"	

(see Binding, pg. 30)

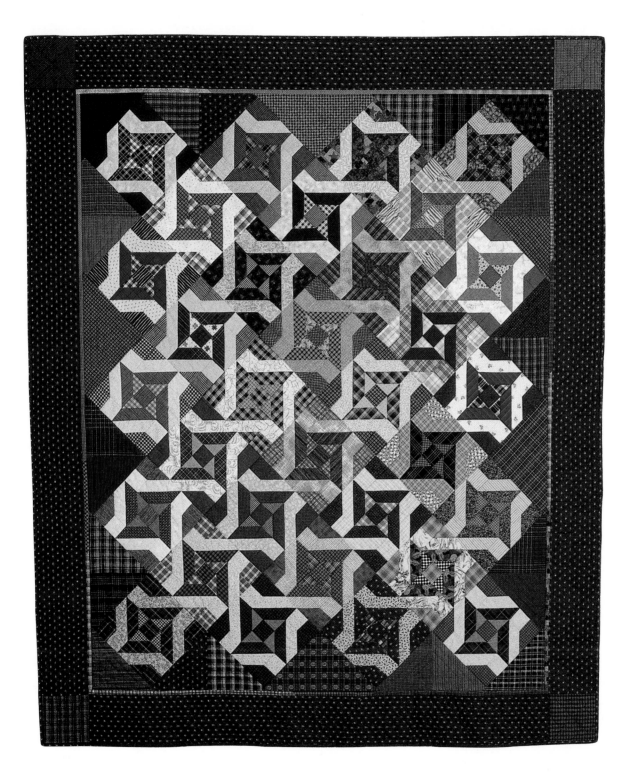

SANDY BAY
(Pieced by Elaine Wright; machine quilted by Bev Dyke)

Elaine had a lot of fun with this scrap version of the same block used in her
TASMAN BAY quilt (pg. 103). But the effect in SANDY BAY was so different. There
is a lot of variation of value in the blocks. Some blocks have more than three
fabrics, so let your imagination fly!

SANDY BAY

Finished size: 70" x 84"
Finished block size: 10"
Number of blocks: 32 (set on point)

Fabric Required
Multi-plaid scraps (minimum per block)
     Lights . . . . 5" x 20"
     Mediums . . . . 2½" x 15"
     Darks . . . . 5" x 30"
Border fabric . . . . 2 yards
Binding. . . . . ⅔ yard or
                 mixed scraps

Basic block

Finished units required for each block

A (x4)   B (x4)   C (x1)

Cutting instructions are for one block.

Unit	Fabric	Minimum scrap size	1ˢᵗ cut	2ⁿᵈ cut	No.	Unit assembly
A	Light	2½" x 10½"	2½"	2½"	4	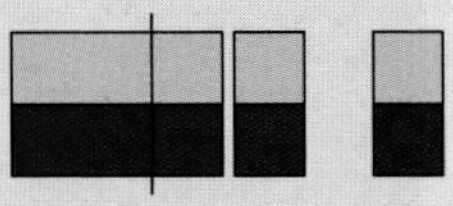
	Dark	2½" x 10½"	2½"	2½"		

• *Sew strips together then cut into 2½" units.*

Unit	Fabric	Minimum scrap size	1ˢᵗ cut	2ⁿᵈ cut	No.	Unit assembly
B	Light	5" x 10"	4⅞"	4⅞"	2	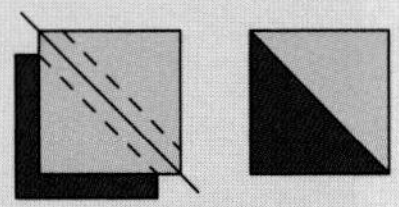
	Dark	5" x 10"	4⅞"	4⅞"	2	
	Medium	2½" x 10"	2½"	2½"	4	
	Dark	2½" x 10"	2½"	2½"	4	

• *Attach one medium Squiffy to the dark side and one dark Squiffy to the light side of Tri-2s as shown.*

• *Join Units A and B.*

Unit	Fabric	Minimum scrap size	1ˢᵗ cut	2ⁿᵈ cut	No.	Unit assembly
C	Medium	2½" x 2½"	2½"	2½"	1	

Uncovering Traditional Quilts – Joyce Jones

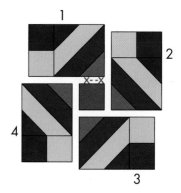

Block Construction

Complete the units then construct the blocks using the Start-a-Seam method as follows:

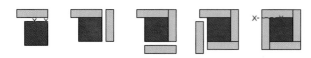
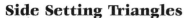
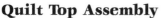

Side Setting Triangles

Use a mixture of the medium to dark plaids found in the blocks. Cut 11½" squares of 14 different fabrics.

Cut each of the 14 squares in half diagonally, then sew them together as shown. Mix most of them but some of them, sew the same fabric back together again.

Quilt Top Assembly

Lay out the blocks, watching for a good flow of color and pattern.

Attach side setting triangles to either end of rows before sewing them together as shown.

Corner Triangles

Cut two 8½" squares of two different fabrics. Cut both squares once diagonally to make four triangles for the corners.

Fold triangles in half to find the center. Pin to the center of the quilt corner before attaching. Trim the corners square.

At this stage in making quilts with side setting triangles, you have a couple of options. The first option is to trim the quilt edges back to the exact measurements given in the instructions and cut border pieces from the instructions.

Quilt assembly diagram

When there isn't a pieced border, my preference is to carefully measure the quilt top and cut the border pieces to fit. In that way, the instructions become guidelines instead of absolutes. Whichever option you take, it is better to always measure across and down the center and check this against the instructions given. In quiltmaking, I find that 2 + 2 can sometimes equal 5.

Measure the quilt down the center and both sides. Cut your scrap strip to the center measurement and sew to fit both sides. Do the same for the top and bottom. If you change this measurement, also remember to change the outer border measurements.

Inner Border

Cut 1" strips of the various light and medium fabrics used in the quilt and sew into strips.

Fabric	1ˢᵗ cut	2ⁿᵈ cut	No.	
Scraps	1"	71"	2	Attach to sides.
Scraps	1"	58"	2	Sew to top and bottom.

Outer Border

Dark	6½"	72"	2	Attach to each side of the quilt top.
Dark	6½"	58"	2	Add corners to each end and attach them to the top and bottom of the quilt.

Corners

Varied	6½"	6½"	4

Quilting

Simple in-the-ditch quilting was used for the blocks. The simple, but effective, border design was based on the shape of the light fabric in the block.

Binding

Medium	2½"	320"	

(see Binding, pg. 30)

SANDY BAY